# Collins

Student Support
Materials for
AQA A2 Psychology

# Unit 3

## Topics in Psychology:
## Aggression

Author and series editor: Mike Cardwell

Published by Collins Education
An imprint of HarperCollins *Publishers*
77–85 Fulham Palace Road
Hammersmith
London
W6 8JB

Browse the complete Collins Education catalogue at www.collinseducation.com

ISBN 978-0-00-742162-6

Mike Cardwell asserts his moral right to be identified as the author of this work.

British Library Cataloguing in Publication Data.
A catalogue record for this publication is available from the British Library.

Commissioned by Charlie Evans and Andrew Campbell
Project managed by Shirley Wakley
Editorial: Hugh Hillyard-Parker
Design and typesetting by G Brasnett, Cambridge
Cover Design by Angela English
Production by Simon Moore
Printed and bound by L.E.G.O. S.p.A. Italy
Indexed by Christine Boylan

**Acknowledgements**
Every effort has been made to contact the holders of copyright material, but if any have been inadvertently overlooked the publishers will be pleased to make the necessary arrangements at the first opportunity.

**Credits and Permissions**
p. 5 (Study), Bandura, A., Ross, D., and Ross, S.A., (1961). 'Transmission of aggression through imitation of aggressive models', *Journal of Abnormal and Social Psychology*, 63, 575–582, Elsevier Science Ltd; p. 9 (Table 2), Watson, R. I. (1973). 'Investigation into deindividuation using a cross-cultural survey technique', *Journal of Personality and Social Psychology*, 25, 342–345, Elsevier Science Ltd; p. 16 (Study), Rosado, B *et al.* (2010). Effect of Fluoxetine on Blood Concentrations of Serotonin, Cortisol and Dehydroepiandrosterone in Canine Aggression. *Journal of Veterinary Pharmacology and Therapeutics*, no. doi: 10.1111/j.1365-2885.2010.01254.x, Elsevier Science Ltd; p. 20 (Study), Book, A.S. *et al.* (2001). 'The Relationship Between Testosterone and Aggression: A Meta-Analysis', *Aggression and Violent Behavior*, 6 (6), 579–599, Elsevier Science Ltd; p. 22 (Study), McBurnett, K. *et al.* (2000). 'Low Salivary Cortisol and Persistent Aggression in Boys Referred for Disruptive Behavior', *Archives of General Psychiatry*, 57, 38–43, American Medical Association; p. 24 (Study), Coccaro, E.F. *et al.* (1997) 'Central serotonin activity and aggression: Inverse relationship with prolactin response to D-fenfluramine, but not CSF 5-HIAA concentration, in human subjects', *American Journal of Psychiatry*, 154:1430–1435, American Psychiatric Association; p. 25 (Study) Miles, D. R. and Carey, G. (1997). Genetic and environmental architecture of human aggression. *Journal of Personality and Social Psychology*, 72, 207–217, Elsevier Science Ltd; p. 29 (Study) Daly, M. and Wilson, M. (1988). 'Evolutionary social psychology and family homicide', *Science* (New Series), 242 (4878), 519–524, American Association for the Advancement of Science.

**Illustrations and photographs**
Cover and p. 1, © Greg Hargreaves/gettyimages.co.uk; p. 11, © Guglielmo Esposito/Rex Features, © George Sweeney/Rex Features; p. 13, © Rex Features; p. 35, © Outdoor-Archiv/Alamy.

# Contents

# Social learning theory

Social psychological theories propose that the causes of aggressive behaviour arise out of our interactions with others in our social world. **Social learning theory** proposes that aggressive behaviour is learned either through direct experience or by vicarious experience, i.e. by observing others and learning from their experiences.

## Direct and vicarious experience

### Traditional learning theory

Learning by direct experience is based on the principles of **operant conditioning**. If aggressive behaviour is reinforced (i.e. produces positive consequences for the individual), it is more likely to occur in similar situations in the future. For example, a child who has a history of successfully bullying other children will attach considerable value to bullying as a method of achieving positive consequences.

### Social learning theory

Children learn to be aggressive by observing the behaviour of those around them, particularly the behaviour of significant others, such as parents or elder siblings. By seeing others being rewarded or punished for their aggressive behaviours, the child experiences **vicarious reinforcement**. From these models, children therefore learn about the nature of aggressive behaviour, the situations where it is appropriate and its likely consequences.

In addition to learning about the likely outcomes of aggressive behaviour, children also develop confidence in their ability to use aggressive behaviour to get what they want. Children who are confident that they will be able to use aggressive behaviour effectively to achieve their ends are high in **self-efficacy**; those with less confidence in their ability to use aggression are low in self-efficacy and may decide to use other methods instead.

## Mental representation of aggressive behaviours

Bandura (1986) claimed that for social learning to take place, individuals must be able to form a mental representation of the aggressive behaviour and the anticipated rewards or punishments that might be associated with it. In the future, if an appropriate opportunity arises, the individual will produce the aggressive behaviour, provided the expectation of reward is greater than the expectation of punishment.

Huesmann (1988) suggests that children learn their aggressive behaviour from aggression models on TV, who become a source of the '**scripts**' that guide the child's own behaviour. These scripts are stored in memory and refined through the individual using these scripts in their own life.

---

**Essential notes**

Aggressive behaviour is learned either by direct reinforcement of aggressive acts or by watching others being rewarded for their aggressive behaviour (vicarious reinforcement).

**Essential notes**

Although aggressive behaviour is learned by direct or vicarious reinforcement, whether it is produced or not is determined by an individual's expectation of reward and confidence in their ability to use it effectively (self-efficacy).

**Examiners' notes**

When describing social learning theory, it is important to describe the theory of social learning rather than concentrating solely on a description of the Bobo doll studies described on the opposite page. Examiners are instructed to award very few marks for answers that describe a study when asked to describe a theory.

# Research on social learning and aggression

Bandura and colleagues carried out a series of experiments involving children being exposed to the aggressive behaviour of an adult model. The main aim of these experiments was to demonstrate:

- a *teaching effect* – whereby the child acquires the behaviour being modelled
- a *motivating effect* – which makes the reproduction of this behaviour more or less likely.

## The Bobo doll studies

Bandura *et al.*'s (1961) experiment involved children watching either aggressive or non-aggressive adult models and then being tested for their imitative behaviour. Half of the children were exposed to an adult model behaving aggressively towards a **Bobo doll** and half exposed to a model who behaved non-aggressively. Following exposure to the models, children were frustrated by being shown, but not allowed to play with, attractive toys. They were then taken to a room where there was a Bobo doll (see Fig. 1).

**Fig. 1**
The Bobo doll used in Bandura's experiments

Children exposed to the aggressive model displayed far more verbal and physical aggression towards the Bobo doll compared to children who had been exposed to the non-aggressive model. Children who had seen a non-aggressive model displayed virtually no aggression towards the doll.

A subsequent experiment (Bandura *et al.* 1963) divided children into three groups. All three watched a film of an adult model behaving aggressively toward a Bobo doll:

- *Group 1* saw an aggressive model who was neither rewarded nor punished for their aggressive behaviour.
- *Group 2* saw an aggressive model who was rewarded by another adult for their aggressive behaviour.
- *Group 3* saw an aggressive model who was punished by another adult for their aggressive behaviour.

Children in Group 2 subsequently behaved most aggressively towards the Bobo doll, whereas children in Group 3 behaved the least aggressively. When offered incentives for each repetition of the model's aggressive behaviour, however, children in Group 3 displayed as many aggressive behaviours as children in Group 2. This demonstrates that all children had *learned* the aggressive behaviours, but only children in Group 2 had been *motivated* to reproduce them.

This topic continues on the next spread. ☞

## Essential notes

The Bobo doll studies established that social learning has a teaching effect, where children learn aggressive behaviours, and a *motivating* effect, where the anticipated consequences of aggressive behaviour determine the likelihood of it being reproduced by the observer.

## Essential notes

Both these studies were laboratory experiments involving manipulation of an **independent variable** (e.g. exposure to an aggressive or non-aggressive model) and subsequent measurement of a **dependent variable** (e.g. number of imitated aggressive acts).

## Examiners' notes

Describing the Bobo doll studies can be a useful way of fleshing out a description of social learning theory, although any such description should be concise and appropriate to the theory point being covered and should be clearly linked to aggression. Alternatively, the studies can be used to support some of the claims being made by the theory (thus becoming part of your *evaluation* of the theory). In this case, you should add something like: 'The theory is supported by evidence from Bandura *et al.*, which showed that...'

## Evaluation of social learning theory

### Explaining inconsistencies in aggressive behaviour

Social learning theory can account for the lack of consistency in people's aggressive behaviour. For example, an individual may behave aggressively at home but not at work. Aggressive behaviour may be more likely to produce positive consequences in one situation (e.g. at home) but not in another (e.g. at work). Consequently, the expectation of the different consequences in these two situations determines the likelihood of aggression being used. This is a strength of social learning theory because it means we can predict whether or not aggressive behaviour is likely in different situations.

### The importance of vicarious reinforcement

Unlike operant conditioning theory, social learning theory can explain why aggressive behaviour can still be learned despite the absence of direct reinforcement. Although the children in Bandura's studies behaved more aggressively after observing an aggressive model, at no point were these children directly reinforced for their own aggressive behaviour. This supports the concept of vicarious reinforcement, that children can acquire behaviours that they see rewarded in others.

### Explaining cultural differences in aggressive behaviour

A further strength of this theory is that it can explain cultural differences in aggressive behaviour. For example, the 'culture of violence' theory proposes that some cultures value (and so model) aggressive behaviour, whereas others value (and therefore model) non-aggressive behaviour.

For example, among the !Kung San people of the Kalahari Desert, aggressive behaviour is rare (Christiansen and Winkler 2006). !Kung San parents do not use physical punishment and aggressive behaviour is devalued in !Kung San society. As a result, the absence of cultural models means there is little opportunity for !Kung San children to learn aggressive behaviour, which would explain its relative absence in this society.

### Social learning or biology?

Biological explanations of aggression have stressed factors that have nothing to do with social learning, but more to do with biological influences, such as the role of hormonal mechanisms. For example, high levels of testosterone have been shown to be linked to aggressive behaviour. Such findings have cast doubt on aggression being purely a learned behaviour.

However, social learning theorists have pointed to societies that exhibit no aggressive behaviour (such as the Amish, a traditional religious denomination known for its simple lifestyle and reluctance to adopt modern convenience) as powerful evidence of the dominant role played by learning rather than biology.

---

**Examiners' notes**

Because marks are given for elaboration of evaluative points, it is a good idea (as here) to identify a point, give the evidence to support that point, and then explain why this is a strength (or weakness) of the theory being evaluated.

---

**Examiners' notes**

When introducing alternative explanations for something (such as aggression), there is always a danger of getting carried away and simply *describing* the alternative explanation. This would not get you many marks. Alternative explanations must be set in context, demonstrating how they offer a challenge to the theory being evaluated.

## Issues, debates and approaches

### Free will versus determinism

The emphasis on 'mental representations' and expectations of reward or punishment might suggest that aggressive behaviour is more a product of an individual's **free will** than of environmental **determinism**. However, according to social learning theory, aggressive behaviour is the product of learning experiences that the child has experienced prior to the actual production of any aggressive behaviours in the future. Consequently, social learning explanations tend to fall on the determinist side of the free will versus determinism debate.

### Cultural differences

The finding that aggressive behaviour is comparatively rare among some people (such as the !Kung San and Amish) constitutes a cultural difference in aggressive behaviour. Demonstrating a cultural difference demonstrates that aggressive behaviour is not universal (i.e. does not apply to everybody) and therefore cannot be solely a product of biology; it must instead be a product of cultural differences in childrearing and other factors that distinguish members of one culture or section of society from another.

### Ethical issues

Concern for the **ethical issues** involved in exposing children to violent behaviour (whether in real life or on film) has meant that studies such as the Bobo doll studies would no longer be allowed. This means that the experimental route to testing experimental hypotheses about the social learning of aggressive behaviour in children has effectively been closed.

## Methodological limitations with the research

### Lack of realism

Social learning theories of aggression rely heavily on experimental studies such as the studies by Bandura and colleagues described earlier. However, there are significant methodological problems with the Bobo doll studies. A Bobo doll is not a living person and does not retaliate when hit, which raises questions as to whether these studies tell us much about the imitation of aggression towards other human beings (who may well retaliate). However, Bandura responded to this criticism by producing a film of an adult hitting a live clown. When the children were subsequently let into the same room as the clown, they proceeded to imitate the same aggressive behaviours they had seen in the film.

### Demand characteristics

It is also possible that the children in Bandura's studies were aware of the behaviour that was expected of them (**demand characteristics**). They may have viewed the films as instructions as to how they should behave. Noble (1975) points out that one child commented to his mother that 'there's the doll we have to hit', indicating that he was responding to what he believed to be appropriate behaviour within the context of the experimental situation. It is possible, therefore, that the children were motivated simply to please the experimenter rather than to be aggressive toward the Bobo doll.

**Examiners' notes**

In order to get anything higher than basic marks for your evaluation, you must include material relating to issues (e.g. gender bias, cultural differences), debates (e.g. free will versus determinism) or approaches (e.g. biological versus behavioural approaches). You will find several examples of how issues, debates and approaches can be integrated successfully into the exam answers in the Exam section. See, for example, p. 43 (fourth paragraph, on ethical issues), p. 44 (fourth paragraph, on gender issues) and p. 59 (second paragraph, on free will vs determinism).

**Examiners' notes**

Be aware that for every question, 9 marks (8 marks after 2012) are available for your descriptive material (AO1) and 16 marks for your evaluative material (AO2). How you construct your answer should reflect this unequal mark allocation, i.e. one-third of your answer should be descriptive material and two-thirds evaluative.

# Deindividuation

## Individuated and deindividuated behaviour

People usually refrain from acting in an aggressive manner because they are easily identifiable and because they belong to societies that have strong norms against aggressive and other forms of antisocial behaviour. Therefore, people are usually in an individuated state (where they believe they are under scrutiny by others and so must act in a socially acceptable manner). However, in certain situations, such as in large crowds, these restraints on aggressive behaviour can become relaxed, so people are more likely to engage in aggressive and antisocial behaviour. When people become faceless and anonymous – as in large crowds – they may enter a deindividuated state, where their behaviour is based on more primitive urges and does not conform to society's norms.

## Research on deindividuation

### Zimbardo (1969)

In this **laboratory experiment**, groups of four female undergraduates were required to deliver electric shocks to another student as an 'aid' to help learning. Zimbardo placed his participants in one of two conditions:

- an individuated condition – e.g. participants wore their normal clothing and a large name badge
- a deindividuated condition – e.g. participants wore bulky lab coats and hoods that covered their heads (see Table 1).

Participants in the deindividuated condition were found to shock the 'learner' for twice as long as participants in the individuated condition.

**Table 1**

Comparison of the two conditions in Zimbardo's (1969) experiment

| Individuated condition | Deindividuated condition |
| --- | --- |
| Participants wore their normal clothing and a large name badge | Participants wore bulky lab coats with hoods and no name badges |
| Instructions were given individually | Instructions given to group rather than individually |
| Participants introduced to each other by name | Participants not introduced to each other |
| Could see each other when seated at shock machines | Could not see each other when seated |

### Deindividuation in real-life studies

Mann (1981) used the concept of deindividuation to explain the antisocial behaviour of mobs. He analysed 21 incidents of suicide jumps reported in US newspapers in the 1960s and 1970s. In ten of these incidents, baiting had occurred, with the crowd urging the potential suicide victim to jump. 'Baiting' tended to occur at night, when the crowd was large and some distance from the person threatening to jump. Mann claimed that these features (darkness, anonymity due to group size and distance) had produced a state of deindividuation, resulting in aggressive behaviour aimed at the suicide victim.

Mullen (1986) analysed newspaper reports of 60 lynchings that had taken place in the first half of the twentieth century. As with the baiting crowd, the more people there were in the lynch mob, the more the deindividuation and the greater the savagery with which members of the crowd killed their victims.

## Deindividuation and intergroup aggression

### Does war paint make people more aggressive?
Anthropologist Robert Watson (1973) tested the hypothesis that warriors who significantly changed their appearance (i.e. entered a deindividuated state) when going to war would be more likely to torture, mutilate and kill their victims, compared to warriors who did not change their appearance when going to war. Watson used data from an anthropological database (the Human Relations Area Files, or HRAF) relating to 23 societies. This indicated the degree to which they changed their appearance (e.g. through the use of war paint or other deindividuating features) and also how they treated their victims.

The results of this analysis showed that, of the 13 societies that showed high levels of aggression towards their victims (that is, they were more likely to kill, torture or mutilate them), all but one of these significantly changed their appearance prior to battle (see Table 2). Of the 10 societies who showed low levels of aggression towards their victims, seven of these did not significantly change their appearance (that is, they were less deindividuated prior to battle).

|        | No change | Changed |
|--------|-----------|---------|
| Low    | 7         | 3       |
| High   | 1         | 12      |

Table 2
Results of Watson's (1973) research into deindividuation and intergroup aggression

### Evaluation: researcher bias
A problem with databases such as the HRAF is that the reports they contain are typically produced by researchers whose cultural experiences and expectations are different from those of the people being studied. Consequently, although these reports may yield some important information about the societies being studied, they may reveal more about the biases and values of the researchers who created them. As a result, these studies may fail to represent accurately the cultures being studied.

### Public and private self-awareness
The concept of deindividuation has been refined to distinguish between the effects of reduced *public* self-awareness (i.e. being anonymous to others) and reduced *private* self-awareness (i.e. focusing less on personal standards of behaviour). Prentice-Dunn and Rodgers (1989) believe that it is a reduction in private self-awareness that is more likely to be associated with various forms of antisocial behaviour, including an increase in aggression.

This topic continues on the next spread. ☞

This topic continues on the next spread. ☞

**Examiners' notes**

As with the comments relating to the Bobo doll studies on an earlier spread, research studies on deindividuation can either be used to expand the descriptive part of an essay (AO1) or as part of the AO2 evaluation. Note how these accounts of studies are merely at a descriptive level, whereas on the next spread, studies will be used as part of a critical (i.e. AO2) commentary.

**Examiners' notes**

Although this research is **anthropological** in nature rather than psychological, it is still relevant as a real-life validation of deindividuation theory.

**Examiners' notes**

Being able to comment on distinctions such as the one between public and private awareness demonstrates a response to the 'stretch and challenge' requirement for more able candidates. In order to access marks in the top bands candidates are expected to explore more abstract complex concepts, address more subtle sensitive issues and extend their critical thinking skills.

## Evaluation of deindividuation theory

### Lack of research support

Although some studies have found support for deindividuation theory's propositions, many have failed to support it, and many have reported contrary results. Even Zimbardo's original study described on page 8 reports that a replication of the study obtained the exact opposite results. A **meta-analysis** of 60 studies of deindividuation (Postmes and Spears 1998) found insufficient support for the main claim that antisocial and aggressive behaviour is more common in large groups or in anonymous settings.

### Deindividuation and prosocial behaviour

Much of the early evidence linked deindividuation and aggressive behaviour, but there is also evidence that deindividuation can also produce increases in **prosocial** rather than antisocial behaviour. This accounts for some apparently contradictory findings that show an increase in prosocial behaviour when people are in a deindividuated state (e.g. expressions of collective good will at religious rallies).

### The importance of local group norms

Johnson and Downing (1979) repeated the Zimbardo study described on page 8, but this time involved deindividuated participants in different ways. One group wore masks and overalls (reminiscent of the Ku Klux Klan, a violent racist group in the USA) and the other group wore nurses' uniforms. The participants shocked more than a control group when dressed in mask and overalls, but less than a control group when dressed in a nurse's uniform. This demonstrates that deindividuation does not necessarily lead to aggressive behaviour, but rather people respond to the **normative cues** associated with the situation in which they find themselves.

### The Zimbardo *et al.* (1973) prison experiment

It is sometimes concluded that the brutality of the guards in Zimbardo's **Stanford Prison Experiment** (SPE) indicates the power of deindividuation to produce aggressive behaviour in even the most psychologically healthy individuals. However, more recent research by Reicher and Haslam (2006) suggests that Zimbardo's participants were acting in terms of *perceived* social roles rather than 'losing their sense of socialized individual identity'. As a result, Zimbardo's experiment may not tell us how real guards behave, but rather how people behave when asked to *act* like guards.

This conclusion is challenged by Zimbardo, who points to the similarities between the behaviour of his guards in the SPE and the behaviour of guards in Abu Ghraib in Iraq (see also p. 13), where much of the aggression against prisoners can be explained in terms of deindividuating factors operating in the prison (e.g. relative anonymity, collective identity of prisoners).

### Essential notes

A meta-analysis is a method of combining the results of lots of studies with the same theme. This enables the researcher to detect any trends in the behaviour being studied.

### Essential notes

These two points emphasize that, although deindividuation can lead to aggressive behaviour, it can also lead to other (non-aggressive) behaviours, depending on situational factors operating at the time.

### Examiners' notes

It is easy to get carried away with a description of Zimbardo's Stanford Prison Experiment. It is essential to stay focused and avoid any needless descriptive content that does not contribute to the evaluative point being developed.

## Issues, debates and approaches

### Gender differences

Research suggests that males and females may not respond in the same way when deindividuated. For example, Cannavale *et al.* (1970) found that males and females tend to respond differently when under conditions of anonymity. An increase in aggression under such conditions was evident in the behaviour of males, but not in females. Thus, evidence suggests that males may be more prone to losing inhibitions concerning aggressive behaviour when in a deindividuated state than females.

### Application to football crowd violence

Stereotyped images of football fans on the rampage suggest a faceless and deindividuated crowd engaged in '…an orgy of aggressive, selfish and antisocial behaviour'. Deindividuation has indeed been described as 'a sense of liberation' because the person tends to live for the moment, taking little responsibility for their actions and feeling safe within the anonymity of the crowd. However, describing football violence as the product of mass deindividuation appears to be an oversimplification. Marsh *et al.* (1978) found that what might appear to be an undisciplined mob can actually consist of several different groups of supporters, each with their own status. They discovered that by serving an 'apprenticeship' of organized aggression over time, young supporters can be 'promoted' into a higher group and can thus continue a 'career' of football violence. In most cases this behaviour is highly ritualized, rather than physically violent.

### Application to violence in Northern Ireland

Silke (2003) examined the relation between anonymity (a key feature that contributes to deindividuation) and aggression in violent assaults that occurred in Northern Ireland over a 30-month period. Information was gathered through media reports, newspapers and from a victim support group. Of the 500 violent attacks analysed as part of this study, 206 were carried out by anonymous individuals who wore disguises to mask their true identities (e.g. balaclavas covering their face, or paramilitary uniforms). There was a significant positive relationship between the use of disguises and different measures of aggression. Disguised offenders were more likely to inflict more serious physical injuries, attack more people at the scene, engage in more acts of vandalism, and were more likely to threaten victims after the attacks.

**Examiners' notes**

There is a requirement in Unit 3 answers to include material relating to 'issues, debates and approaches'. Applications to real life (e.g. football crowd violence) would satisfy this requirement in this context, although you need to introduce any such material by emphasizing the application (and therefore relevance) of this theory to understanding real-life problems.

Football violence: a case of mass deindividuation or highly ritualized behaviour?

**Examiners' notes**

An 'elaborated' critical point (see p. 39) would ideally be about 50–60 words. Therefore, each of the two applications detailed on this page should be distilled down to this word count in order to give the gist of what is being said.

# Institutional aggression

**Institutional aggression** can take many forms. 'Institutions' may be distinct entities (such as schools or prisons) or may involve a whole society or sections within that society. Acts of institutional aggression range from the physical abuse of individuals during initiation rituals (e.g. when new recruits join an army unit) to acts designed to destroy a national, racial or religious group (genocide).

## Institutional aggression in prisons

### The importation model (Irwin and Cressey 1962)

This model claims that some people who enter prison do so already possessing certain characteristics (i.e. values, attitudes and experiences) that predispose them toward interpersonal violence within prison. According to this explanation of institutional aggression, interpersonal violence is not a product of the institution itself (i.e. any 'violent' characteristics of the prison environment), but rather of the characteristics of those violent individuals who enter such institutions.

Statistics suggest that young inmates have a more difficult time adjusting to prison; therefore, they are more likely to have confrontations with other inmates and with prison staff, and are more likely to view violence as an appropriate way to deal with conflicts within prison.

Research in the US has shown that Black inmates are more likely to be associated with interpersonal violence than are White inmates. An explanation typically offered for this is that more Black prisoners enter prison from impoverished communities with higher rates of violent crime. As a result, they are more likely to bring (i.e. import) into prison the cultural norms that condone violent behaviour.

### The deprivation model (Sykes 1958)

This model claims that it is the characteristic of the prison itself rather than the prison population that accounts for violence in prisons. Proponents of this model argue that it is primarily the *experience* of imprisonment that causes extreme stress and frustration for inmates and this, in turn, leads to violence against other inmates or members of prison staff.

Sykes (1958) commented on those factors that are part of the prison experience for inmates and that might be expected to contribute to interpersonal violence as a response. They include the loss of freedom, boredom, discomfort and loneliness. Social psychological research also suggests that other factors that are a common part of the prison experience would also be more likely to contribute to violence among inmates. These include heat, noise and overcrowding. For example, the overcrowding crisis in UK prisons has forced many inmates to share cells, and this is linked to an increase in interpersonal violence.

### The power of the situation

Zimbardo (2007) emphasizes that the situation can have a powerful influence on people's willingness to inflict harm on others. In his Stanford

## Essential notes

Institutional violence refers to violent behaviour that exists *within* – and may be a defining feature of – certain institutions or groups. It can also refer to other forms of collective violence between social groups based on the racial, national or religious characteristics of members of one group.

## Examiners' notes

Responses to questions that ask for *explanations* of institutional aggression can be limited to just these two explanations of institutional aggression in prisons, or may include Zimbardo's work on the role of situational, dehumanizing factors that contribute to aggression in some situations (see p. 8).

Prison Experiment (SPE), Zimbardo showed how institutional factors, such as lack of external constraints and peer pressure, led the 'guards' to disregard the potential harm of their actions towards the 'prisoners'. In these conditions, claims Zimbardo, individuals are at greater risk of deviating from societal norms of acceptable conduct.

## Institutional aggression in a real-life setting

Zimbardo claims that the same social psychological processes that were found in the SPE were also apparent during the abuse of Iraqi prisoners at the Abu Ghraib prison. These included deindividuation, **dehumanization**, group conformity and lack of supervision. As with the 'guards' in the SPE, these processes led to a diminished sense of accountability from the guards responsible for the abuse. Zimbardo believes that institutional aggression depends much on circumstances, in particular the external influences found in the SPE and in Abu Ghraib. These external influences also extend to the system itself, i.e. those who create the potentially abusive environments found in places such as Abu Ghraib.

**Essential notes**

Zimbardo makes the general point that the causes of institutional aggression do not arise from within the individual (i.e. the idea of 'bad apples in a barrel'), but rather it is the situation itself (i.e. the bad barrel) that corrupts everything that comes into contact with it. Hence, it is the situation that leads to institutional aggression in individuals who are exposed to those influences.

Abu Ghraib prison in Iraq – an example of institutional aggression

## Institutional aggression between groups: The effect of dehumanizing labels

Zimbardo (2007) argues that people are more likely to be aggressive when they dehumanize or label others in a way that removes the moral constraints that usually inhibit violent behaviour against other human beings. For example, in an experiment by Bandura *et al.* (1975), participants overheard an assistant refer to students from another school as 'animals', while in another condition, these students were referred to as 'nice'. When later required to deliver what they thought were real electric shocks to the other students, higher shocks were given in the 'animal' condition.

**Essential notes**

Although human beings usually have moral inhibitions about killing other human beings, this changes if the target group is dehumanized so that its members are seen as worthless animals and therefore not worthy of the sort of moral consideration normally reserved for fellow humans.

Institutional aggression resulting from dehumanization is not restricted to laboratory experiments but is evident in real-life conflicts as well. In the Rwandan genocide in 1994, the influential Hutu-controlled 'hate radio' station RTLM encouraged other Hutus to turn against their Tutsi neighbours by referring to them as 'inyenzi' (cockroaches).

This topic continues on the next spread. ☞

# Evaluation of explanations of institutional aggression

### Research support for the importation model

Harer and Steffensmeier (1996) analysed data from 58 US prisons and found that Black inmates displayed significantly *higher* levels of violent behaviour but lower rates of alcohol and drug misconduct compared to White inmates. They concluded that these differences reflected racial differences in these behaviours in US society generally, supporting the claim that such characteristics are imported into the prison environment.

### Research contradicting the importation model

The importation model predicts that membership of a violent gang prior to imprisonment would result in increased levels of violence in prison, as violent conduct would be imported to the new environment. However, this prediction is not supported by research. A study of over 800 male inmates (DeLisi *et al.* 2004) found no evidence that membership of a violent gang prior to prison had any bearing on levels of violence within prison.

### Research support for the deprivation model

Many of the claims of the deprivation model are supported by research evidence. For example, McCorkle *et al.* (1995) found that overcrowding, lack of privacy and a lack of meaningful activity in prison all significantly influence interpersonal violence. Likewise, Light (1990) found that when overcrowding in prisons increases, so do the levels of violence.

### Research challenging the deprivation model

The deprivation model is challenged by the findings of research by Poole and Regoli (1983). They found that among juvenile offenders in four different institutions, pre-institutional violence was the best predictor of inmate aggression *regardless* of the particular features (e.g. overcrowding, discomfort) of the institution. This finding supports the importation model and casts doubt on the validity of the deprivation model as an explanation of institutional aggression.

### Relevance of the deprivation model to the 21st century

The deprivation model might not be particularly applicable today because many of the deprivations originally described by Sykes in 1958 have been reduced considerably as a result of prison reform and the inmate rights movement. An increased emphasis on training, education and other meaningful activities, as well as an increasing provision of anger management courses in prison, has decreased the deprivations experienced by prisoners in UK prisons. Despite this, however, the levels of violence remain high, suggesting that much of this violence can be attributed to prisoner characteristics prior to confinement.

# Issues, debates and approaches

## Ethnic differences in institutional aggression
Gaes *et al.* (2002) conducted a study of inmate violence using the entire male inmate population in the US, a sample that exceeded 82 000 cases. Several important findings emerged, including the finding that, regardless of citizenship, Hispanics (i.e. Americans with origins in the *Hispanic* countries of Latin America or Spain) were more violent prisoners than non-Hispanics. On the other hand, inmates of Asian descent were less likely than other prisoners to engage in serious violent behaviour. Thus, ethnicity appeared to be a powerful correlate of prisoner violence, supporting the importation model of institutional aggression.

## Applications of the deprivation model to institutional aggression in modern prisons
In 1998, criminologist and former prison governor David Wilson designed and managed two special units for the 12 most violent prisoners in the UK at HMP Woodhill. Wilson argued that most violence occurs in environments that are hot, noise-polluted (e.g. lots of shouting, banging of cell doors) and overcrowded – that is, in situations where conditions contribute to the 'deprivation' of prison life.

By changing the levels of noise, heat and crowding at Woodhill, there was a dramatic decrease in violent conduct among these prisoners. This supports the deprivation model because, despite these violent prisoners being 'imported' into Woodhill, it was situational changes that led to a change in their aggressive behaviour.

## Links between psychopathology and institutional aggression
Baskin *et al.* (1991) examined the link between different forms of **psychopathology** and several types of prison violence. Controlling for background and other possible causes of institutional aggression, the study found that certain forms of psychiatric impairment increased the probability of violent behaviour within the prison context. They found that:
- depression was related to self-directed violence
- confusion increased violence towards other inmates and staff
- depression and confusion together increased violence towards property.

The research suggests that mental-health risk factors are associated with prison violence, and so supports the importation model.

**Essential notes**

Ethnic differences, particularly when demonstrated on such a large scale, are significant because they suggest that inmates 'import' violent characteristics based on their ethnic background. The cause of these characteristics (genetics, socialization, etc.) is relatively unimportant. What is important is that these characteristics are present upon entry into the prison system and are influential in the causes of subsequent interpersonal aggression while in prison.

**Examiners' notes**

Making connections between different areas of the specification (in this case between 'aggression' and 'psychopathology') is evidence of the skill of 'synopticity', and will be credited as part of the AO2/AO3 requirements of any question in this area.

# Neural mechanisms in aggression

The neural mechanisms that are most associated with aggressive behaviour are **neurotransmitters**. Two neurotransmitters are believed to be important in the control of aggressive behaviour. *Low* levels of **serotonin** and *high* levels of **dopamine** are associated with aggressive behaviour.

**Essential notes**

Neurotransmitters are chemicals that allow impulses in one area of the brain to be transmitted to another area. Therefore, all behaviours, including aggression, are influenced by the action of neurotransmitters.

## Serotonin

### How does serotonin influence aggression?

Serotonin, in normal levels, exerts a calming, inhibitory effect on neuronal firing in the brain. Low levels of serotonin, particularly in the prefrontal cortex, remove this inhibitory effect with the consequence that individuals are less able to control their impulsive and aggressive behaviour. Under normal circumstances, serotonin works in the frontal areas of the brain to inhibit the firing of the **amygdala**, the part of the brain that controls fear, anger and other emotional responses. However, if there is less serotonin in these frontal areas of the brain, there is less inhibition of the amygdala. As a result, when the amygdala is stimulated by external (and potentially threatening) events, it becomes more active, causing the person to act on their impulses, and making aggression more likely.

### Support for the serotonin–aggression link

Support for the role of serotonin in aggressive behaviour comes from a number of different sources:

- *Metabolite levels* – The major metabolite (waste product) of serotonin tends to be low in the cerebrospinal fluid of people who display aggressive behaviour (Brown *et al.* 1982). The lack of waste products associated with the breakdown of serotonin is an indirect indication of low levels of serotonin in many aggressive individuals.
- *Dexfenfluramine* – Levels of serotonin have been manipulated in order to see if this results in changes in aggressive thoughts or behaviours. Mann *et al.* (1990) administered the drug dexfenfluramine (which depletes serotonin in the brain) to 35 healthy adults. The researchers used a questionnaire to assess hostility and aggression levels, which rose following administration of dexfenfluramine among males (but not among females).
- *Studies of antisocial individuals* – Scerbo and Raine (1993) carried out a meta-analysis of 29 studies that had examined serotonin levels in antisocial children and adults. These studies consistently found lower levels of serotonin than normal in these individuals. This was particularly the case in individuals who had attempted suicide, which suggests that serotonin depletion leads to impulsive behaviour, making aggressive behaviour (including suicide) more likely.
- *Evidence from animal studies* – Rosado *et al.* (2010) took blood samples from 80 dogs referred to veterinary hospitals because of their aggressive behaviour toward humans. They compared these samples with blood samples taken from non-aggressive dogs. The aggressive dogs averaged 278 units of serotonin, while the non-aggressive dogs averaged 387 units of serotonin.

**Examiners' notes**

There is more than enough descriptive material on these two pages to address a question that is *entirely* on neural mechanisms in aggressive behaviour. However, far more likely are questions that require explanations of both neural *and* hormonal mechanisms, or parted questions that offer only a proportion of the 25 marks (2009 onwards) or 24 marks (2012 onwards) available for coverage of neural mechanisms. Either way, you will need to get used to paraphrasing this material; so, using the material on these two pages, construct a 200-word précis (for 9/8 marks) and also a 100-word précis (for 5/4 marks).

# Dopamine

Although not as well established as the link with serotonin, there is some evidence that dopamine does have some influence on aggressive behaviour, with increases in dopamine being associated with increases in aggressive behaviour.

## How does dopamine influence aggression?

Recent evidence with mice (Couppis *et al.* 2008) suggests that the brain appears to see aggression as a reward. According to this view, whenever we perform an activity that we find rewarding (e.g. sex, eating or recreational drugs), the brain releases higher levels of dopamine. When this dopamine attaches to receptors in the brain, it creates a pleasure circuit, which the individual finds reinforcing. The person is thus motivated to repeat the actions that led to this increase in dopamine, which may then make aggressive behaviour (i.e. either performing or watching) more frequent.

## Support for the dopamine–aggression link

Support for the role of dopamine in aggressive behaviour also comes from a number of different sources:

- *Schizophrenia and the use of antipsychotics* – Increased rates of violence are sometimes found in **schizophrenia**, usually when the patient is severely delusional, resists taking their medication and has a past history of violence. As dopamine dysfunction is implicated in schizophrenia, this has led to the view that increased levels of dopamine activity are somehow associated with aggressive behaviour. As a result, antipsychotics, which reduce dopamine levels, have been suggested as an intervention in the treatment of aggressive behaviour and have been effectively used in decreasing violence in both non-psychotic and psychotic populations (e.g. Glazer and Dickson 1998).
- *Amphetamines* – Increases of dopamine activity via the usage of **amphetamines** have been associated with aggressive behaviour. Much of this evidence is anecdotal (for example, studies of prison violence have discovered that a large proportion of inmates commit violent acts while 'high' on amphetamines). However, there is also some experimental evidence for this link. Cherek *et al.* (1986) administered either amphetamines or caffeine to participants in a competitive laboratory task, and found amphetamines *raised* the frequency of interpersonal hostility whereas caffeine *reduced* it.
- *Evidence from animal studies* – van Erp and Miczek (2000) measured dopamine levels in the **prefrontal cortex** of male rats before, during, and after a confrontation with another rat. They found a significant increase in dopamine levels over baseline levels after the confrontation, suggesting that increased levels of dopamine are not a *cause* of aggressive behaviour, but a *response* to it.

## Essential notes

Unlike serotonin, which appears to have a causal link with aggressive behaviour, the link with dopamine is less clear cut. Research suggests that the link may involve raised levels of dopamine as a *consequence* of aggression rather than a *cause* of it.

## Examiners' notes

Marks for AO1 description are awarded on a variety of criteria in questions. These include *accuracy* (e.g. having the lowered/raised link the right way around for serotonin and dopamine), *detail* (e.g. fleshing out your answer with some of the 'support for' information on these pages), and *breadth/depth*. This last criterion requires a balance between how much information you present (breadth) and how much detail you go into with each point. It is advantageous to go for a balance of these rather than going solely for breadth (or depth) alone.

This topic continues on the next spread. ☞

## Evaluation of neural mechanisms in aggression

### Examiners' notes

If you introduce an alternative explanation as part of your evaluation, you must do more than just describe it. In order to make it part of a critical commentary, you need to consider how this explanation fits in with whatever you are attempting to evaluate. Sometimes (as here) it can be as simple as pointing out the subtle difference between the two explanations that might offer a better explanation for the same findings.

### Essential notes

Booij *et al.* suggested that the *reason* for low-serotonin adults not showing high levels of aggression (as we might expect) is because psychological and cognitive factors that develop with age tend to buffer these individuals from their increased risk for aggressive behaviour due to their low serotonin levels.

### Serotonin: alternative explanations

It is possible that aggression is not caused by low levels of serotonin in the brain, but by low **serotonin metabolism**. If **presynaptic neurons** do not release enough neurotransmitter into the synapse (low serotonin metabolism), then there is a corresponding increase in the number of **post-synaptic receptors** as the brain attempts to compensate for this deficiency. Evidence for this comes from the finding that among suicide 'completers' (i.e. people who succeed in killing themselves), those with increased numbers of serotonin receptors in the prefrontal cortex had chosen more violent methods of suicide (Mann *et al.* 1996).

### Environment and neurotransmitter interactions

Although low serotonin levels have been linked to an increase in aggressive behaviour, not all people with low levels of this neurotransmitter display aggressive behaviour, so other factors must play a part in the determination of aggressive behaviour. Booij *et al.* (2010) carried out a **longitudinal study** that followed individuals throughout childhood and into adulthood. They measured aggression through parental and self-reports and serotonin synthesis through **PET scans**. As expected, children with low levels of serotonin displayed higher levels of aggressive behaviour than children with normal serotonin levels. However, by the time these children reached adulthood, they showed no difference in aggression levels compared to normal controls *despite* the fact that their serotonin levels remained low.

### Alcohol, serotonin and aggressive behaviour

Badawy (2006) found that alcohol consumption caused major disturbances in the metabolism of brain serotonin, depleting serotonin levels in the brains of normal individuals. In susceptible individuals, this depletion of serotonin can lead to aggressive behaviour in response to environmental or psychological stimuli.

### Research support

Ferrari *et al.* (2003) provided support for the role of both serotonin *and* dopamine in aggressive behaviour. They allowed a rat to fight with another rat at a specific time every day for ten days. On the eleventh day, the rat was not allowed to fight, but instead the researchers measured the levels of dopamine and serotonin in the rat's brain. They found that, in anticipation of the imminent fight, the rat's dopamine levels had *increased* and its serotonin levels had *decreased*, despite the fact that it did not actually fight. This shows that experience had changed the rat's brain chemistry, altering it in ways that would be consistent with the onset of aggressive behaviour.

### Difficulties of establishing a link between dopamine and aggression

Studying the link between dopamine and aggressive behaviour *experimentally* poses special problems for the researcher. Studies using mice (e.g. Couppis *et al.* 2008) investigate the effects of dopamine by 'turning off' dopamine in the animal's brain. However, dopamine also has an important role in the coordination of movement. Therefore, any resulting decrease in the animal's aggressive behaviour may be due to a decreased motivation to be aggressive or simply that the animal finds it difficult to move.

## Issues, debates and approaches

### Reductionism and neural explanations
The link between neurotransmitters and aggression largely ignores the important role played by social factors in aggression. For example, research by Bandura *et al.* (1961, 1963) (see p. 5) has shown that social learning can be a powerful influence on the aggressive behaviour of children, and Zimbardo *et al.* (1973) (see p. 10) has described how deindividuation can increase aggressive behaviour in particular situations where personal responsibility is diminished. Reductionist explanations of human aggression underestimate the complexity of aggressive behaviour and are insufficient on their own to explain the many different aspects of human aggressive behaviour.

### Evidence from non-human animal studies
The link between neural mechanisms and aggression is well established in non-human animals; however, the link is less clear in human beings. A major challenge to the belief that research on animals can easily be generalized to humans, was provided by the *Seville Statement on Violence* (1986). In this statement, scientists from 12 different countries formally challenged a number of popular beliefs based on scientific findings with animals and humans that had been used to justify violent behaviour in humans. This included the notion that human aggression is inherited, or instinctual, or could be reduced to the action of neurochemicals as suggested by animal models of aggression.

### Real-world application: treating aggressive behaviour
If aggressive behaviour is a product of decreased levels of serotonin in the brain, then it should be possible to treat aggression by administering an **SSRI** antidepressant drug, which would increase the amount of serotonin available in the synapse. These drugs are being used effectively to control violent behaviour in selective groups, e.g. elderly patients with dementia living in residential nursing homes, and aggressive children. For example, a study by Ghaziuddin and Alessi (1992) found that administration of the antidepressant trazodone produced a notable improvement in about half of the children treated.

**Essential notes**
Studies using non-human animals can offer a direct way of exploring the influence of a particular neurotransmitter – it can simply be 'turned off' and the results noted. However, we need to remember that aggressive behaviour in rodents is a far less complex behaviour than in humans. Human behaviour involves many other factors, which makes its investigation far more complicated and any conclusions that might be drawn far more tentative.

**Examiners' notes**
If you choose to write about animal studies as part of your AO2 evaluation, it should be to make the point (as here) concerning the validity of using animal studies to inform explanations of human aggression. Discussion of the ethics of animal studies would not be relevant in this context.

# Hormonal mechanisms in aggression

## Testosterone and aggression

Testosterone is one of the **androgen hormones**, so called because they produce male characteristics (which is why aggression is often seen as more of a male characteristic). Levels of testosterone reach a peak in young adult males and typically these levels gradually decline with age.

### Evidence for the testosterone and aggression link

The nature of the link between testosterone and aggression is not a simple cause-and-effect mechanism. Rather, the action of testosterone on brain areas involved in controlling aggression makes it more likely that a particular behaviour will be displayed. Evidence for the association between testosterone and aggression comes from a number of sources:

- Archer (1991) carried out a meta-analysis of five studies (involving 230 male adults) and found a low positive correlation between levels of testosterone and aggression.
- A larger meta-analysis of 45 studies (Book *et al.* 2001) found an average correlation of +0.14 between testosterone and aggression.
- Olweus *et al.* (1988) compared samples of delinquent boys and non-delinquent male students. They found higher levels of testosterone in the delinquent sample, although this was not statistically significant. Delinquents with a history of violent offences also had higher levels of testosterone than those with a history of non-violent offences.
- Strong evidence for the role of testosterone in influencing aggression comes from animal studies. Research that has used the hormone removal (through castration) and testosterone replacement approach has shown a definite link between testosterone and aggression in animals. In general, this research has found that castration leads to a decrease in aggression in animals whilst replacement of testosterone restores the behaviour (Edwards 1969).

### The challenge hypothesis (Wingfield *et al.* 1990)

This proposes that, in **monogamous** species, testosterone levels should only rise above a baseline level in response to social challenges, such as male–male aggression or threats to status. As humans are essentially monogamous, we might therefore expect male testosterone levels to rise sharply in response to such challenges, particularly those which are considered threats to reproductive success. The challenges may be direct (e.g. a dispute over a female) or indirect (e.g. a dispute over resources or status), both of which are linked to reproductive success in humans. According to this explanation, therefore, competitive encounters between young men would lead to a surge in testosterone levels.

## Cortisol and aggression

Van Goozen *et al.* (2007) claim that there is a link between aggression and the hormone **cortisol**. They believe that the relationship between cortisol and aggression is an **inverse correlation**, as *lower* levels of cortisol are associated with *higher* levels of aggressive behaviour.

## Essential notes

Hormones are chemicals (such as testosterone and cortisol) that regulate and control bodily functions.

## Examiners' notes

Research 'evidence' can play a dual role in essay questions in this area, depending on your need. For example, if you need material to bolster your AO1 description, then you simply describe one or more of the studies on the right. However, it is easy enough to turn this material into AO2 evaluation by simply building a critical point around the study. For example, the Book *et al.* meta-analysis could be rephrased thus: 'The link between testosterone and aggression is supported by Book *et al.* (2001), who carried out a meta-analysis of 45 studies and found an average correlation of +0.14 between testosterone and aggression.'

## Essential notes

Cortisol is produced by the adrenal gland and is an important part of the body's reaction to stress.

## Explanations of the cortisol–aggression link

Cortisol appears to have an important mediating influence on other aggression-related hormones such as testosterone, by inhibiting the likelihood of aggressive behaviour. A study by Popma *et al.* (2006) found a significant positive relationship between testosterone and aggression, but only in participants with low cortisol levels. The relationship did not exist in participants with high cortisol levels.

An alternative explanation of this link is that low autonomic nervous system (ANS) arousal (and therefore low cortisol levels) is experienced as being aversive (unpleasant). As a result, aggressive behaviour becomes an attempt to create a stressful situation in order to provoke ANS activation and cortisol release.

## Evidence for the cortisol and aggression link

Evidence for a link between cortisol and aggression has come from various research studies:

- Virkunnen (1985) found that antisocial adults tend to have low resting levels of cortisol. In particular, he found that offenders with antisocial personality disorder *and* a habitually violent tendency had lower cortisol levels than individuals with antisocial personality disorder who displayed aggressive behaviour only occasionally.
- Fairchild and Goodyer (2008) discovered that males who display antisocial behaviours such as aggression tend to have significantly lower levels of cortisol than their better-behaved peers. They compared the cortisol levels of both groups in a neutral setting and again in a stressful situation. Among the non-antisocial boys, cortisol levels rose dramatically during the stressful situation, whereas among the antisocial boys, their cortisol levels dropped significantly. This resulted in an inability to inhibit inappropriate responses to the stressful situation, including aggression.
- In a study of conduct disorder, Reinecke (2011) examined cortisol levels in pre-school children to see whether they predicted concurrent (in pre-school) and later (in kindergarten) aggression. Basal cortisol (i.e. base rate level of cortisol) was measured in saliva samples collected on two mornings and reactive cortisol (i.e. in response to stress) collected over the course of a series of challenging tasks. Teachers provided ratings of later child aggression. Lower basal cortisol in pre-school predicted higher aggression in kindergarten a year later. Among the kindergarten children, lowered levels of cortisol during the challenging tasks were also associated with higher aggression ratings.

### Essential notes

Conduct disorder is marked by a pattern of behaviour where social norms are violated, the symptoms of which include verbal and physical aggression, cruel behaviour towards other people and pets, and generally destructive behaviour.

This topic continues on the next spread. ☞

# Evaluation of hormonal mechanisms in aggression

### Inconsistent evidence on the testosterone–aggression link

The relationship between testosterone and aggression is far from clear cut. A number of studies (e.g. Archer 1991) have found that high testosterone levels correlate positively with high levels of aggression, but other studies (e.g. Bain *et al.* 1987) have found no such relationship. Bain and colleagues found no significant difference in testosterone levels between men who had been charged with murder or violent assault, and men who had been charged with non-violent crimes such as burglary.

In addition, most of the studies that *do* show a positive correlation between testosterone and aggression have involved relatively small samples of males within prison populations, using either self-reports of aggression, or measures of aggression that are assumed from the type or severity of the crime involved.

### Aggression or dominance?

Mazur (1985) argues that we should distinguish between aggression and **dominance** (having status over or controlling other individuals). Aggression is more likely when the intent is to inflict injury on another human being, whereas individuals display dominance behaviour if their intent is to achieve or maintain status over the other individual. Mazur claims that aggression is only one form of dominance behaviour, and that the influence of testosterone on dominance may be evident in many more subtle ways that do not include aggression. This may well explain why some studies find a positive association between testosterone and aggression whereas others do not.

### The positive influence of testosterone

Zitzmann (2006) argues that not only is the link between testosterone and aggression not proven, but that testosterone may also have many positive effects for males. Testosterone supplements have been shown to increase energy and vigour in older males and low levels of testosterone are linked with depression in older males (Barrett-Connor *et al.* 1999). Increases in positive mood and decreases in negative mood were confirmed following testosterone replacement therapy in a study of 208 men with testosterone deficiency (McNicholas *et al.* 2003). Testosterone has also been shown to have positive effects on women's wellbeing. Davis (2000) found that testosterone was important in maintaining a woman's energy level and sense of wellbeing, regardless of her age.

### Research support for the cortisol–aggression link

Support for an inverse relationship between cortisol and aggression is evident in a number of longitudinal studies. McBurnett *et al.* (2000) evaluated 38 boys who had been referred to a clinic with behavioural problems. The children's behaviours were evaluated annually for a period of four years. They found that boys with consistently low cortisol levels began carrying out antisocial acts at an earlier age and had three times the number of aggressive symptoms compared to boys with high or fluctuating cortisol levels. The boys with low cortisol levels were also consistently named as being the most aggressive and the 'meanest' by their peers, thus providing real-life support for the link between cortisol and aggression.

### Inconsistent evidence on the cortisol–aggression link
Although some studies have found evidence of lower cortisol levels in aggressive samples, other studies have found no significant differences between aggressive samples and controls. Some studies (e.g. Gerra *et al.* 1997) have even reported *higher* cortisol levels in adolescents during experimentally induced aggression.

Methodological issues may explain these inconsistencies in research findings. Sampling cortisol from saliva is the usual method, with many studies relying on a single cortisol measurement only. Different studies sample at different times of the day, which may have influenced results considerably because cortisol levels fluctuate naturally over a 24-hour period.

## Issues, debates and approaches

### Gender bias
Most of what we know about the relationship between testosterone and aggression is based on studies of males. Currently there is little research that has explored the relationship between testosterone and aggression in females. Research suggests that the association between testosterone and aggression may be even higher among females (Archer *et al.* 2005). Other research (Baucom *et al.* 1985) has found that women with higher testosterone levels had higher occupational status, possibly as a result of being more assertive. Studies such as this also report that these women tend to respond to challenging situations with increased levels of testosterone, with an associated rise in traits such as aggressiveness and dominance.

### Real-world application
The link between testosterone and aggression has been used to inform the argument why the presence of guns in the environment may increase aggression. The presence of certain stimuli, such as guns or knives, trigger increases in testosterone, which in turn may lead to increases in aggressive behaviour.

To test this hypothesis, Klinesmith *et al.* (2006) allowed male college students to handle either a gun or a child's toy for 15 minutes. A comparison of saliva samples taken before and after this activity showed that students who had handled the gun showed significantly greater increases in testosterone and displayed more aggressive behaviour towards another participant compared to the students who played with the child's toy.

**Examiners' notes**

In all Unit 3 questions, there is a requirement for some issues, debates or approaches (IDA) content. Therefore, although you can be selective about which of the points on these two pages that you choose to address the AO2 requirement of the question, you should include at least one of the IDA points included here.

**Essential notes**

Studies of the relationship between testosterone and aggression have tended to use males because they produce far more testosterone than females. As a result, the hormone is easier to measure and its effects are therefore clearer in males than in females.

# Genetic factors in aggressive behaviour

Researchers have approached the investigation of genetic factors in aggressive behaviour in a number of different ways to try and establish whether aggression is more a product of inherited characteristics (nature) or environmental influences (nurture).

Methods include twin and adoption studies as well as a search for individual genes that may influence the development of aggressive behaviour.

## Twin studies

**Essential notes**

Monozygotic (MZ) twins share all their genes, whereas dizygotic twins (DZ) share only 50 per cent of their genes.

If a researcher compares the similarity between sets of MZ twins to the similarity between sets of DZ twins for a trait such as aggression and finds that MZ twins are more alike in terms of this trait, then this extra similarity is assumed to be due to genetic factors. In humans, research has generally found that aggressive behaviour is more highly correlated in MZ twins than in DZ twins.

### Twin study research

McGuffin and Gottesman (1985) found a **concordance rate** of 87 per cent for aggressive and antisocial behaviour for MZ pairs, compared with 72 per cent for DZ pairs.

A meta-analysis by Mason and Frick (1994) of 12 twin studies concluded that approximately 50 per cent of the difference between antisocial and non-antisocial behaviours could be attributed to genetic factors, with larger estimates of genetic influence found for more violent behaviours.

Coccaro *et al.* (1997) analysed data from 182 male MZ twin pairs and 118 male DZ twin pairs. From this data they estimated that genes accounted for more than 40 per cent of the individual differences in all types of aggression. This figure was higher for individual differences in physical aggression (50 per cent) and lower for individual differences in verbal aggression (30 per cent).

## Adoption studies

A second way of studying the influence of genetic factors is by studying children who have been brought up by parents who are not their *biological* parents. If researchers find a greater similarity in levels of aggression between adopted children and their biological parents than between adopted children and their adoptive parents, then this suggests an important *genetic* influence is at work. If, however, the children are more similar to their adoptive parents (with whom they share no genes) than to their biological parents, then this suggests that *environmental* influences are more important.

### Adoption study research

Hutchings and Mednick (1973) reviewed over 14 000 adoptions in Denmark. They found a significant positive correlation between the number of convictions for criminal violence among the biological parents (particularly the fathers) and the number of convictions for criminal violence among their adopted sons.

Miles and Carey (1997) carried out a meta-analysis of 24 twin and adoption studies concerned with the genetic basis of aggression. They found a strong genetic influence, which accounted for about 50 per cent of the variance in aggression in both types of study. A more recent meta-analysis (Rhee and Waldman 2002) found approximately a 40 per cent genetic influence for antisocial behaviour, which included delinquency and behavioural aggression. They found little evidence of any gender differences in the findings.

## Genes for aggression

Researchers have identified a number of '**candidate genes**' that are thought to contribute to an increased risk of engaging in antisocial and aggressive behaviour.

### DRD4 and DRD3

Dysfunctions of serotonin and dopamine are known to increase aggressiveness; therefore, genes that are associated with the expression of these neurotransmitters are also considered to influence aggressive behaviour indirectly. A meta-analysis by Faraone *et al.* (2001) of studies of the gene for the dopamine receptor D4 (DRD4) found a modest association between variants of this gene and attention deficit hyperactivity disorder (**ADHD**). The relationship between ADHD and aggressive behaviour has been consistently demonstrated in research (e.g. Zepf *et al.* 2008). Other studies have concentrated on the gene for dopamine receptor D3 (DRD3). Retz *et al.* (2003) found an association between a variant of the DRD3 gene and both **impulsivity** and ADHD symptoms in violent offenders.

### Monoamine oxidase A (MAOA)

Researchers have found that the gene for MAOA may also be associated with individual differences in aggressive behaviour. MAOA breaks down neurotransmitters such as noradrenaline and dopamine after they have transmitted an impulse from one nerve cell to another. Brunner *et al.* (1993) studied a family in the Netherlands, many of whose male members behaved in a particularly violent and aggressive manner. These violent individuals were found to have abnormally low levels of MAOA in their bodies.

Brunner and colleagues reasoned that if these men were suffering from defective MAOA, excess levels of the neurotransmitters (such as dopamine and noradrenaline) that are normally broken down by this enzyme would accumulate in their bodies. They believe that the excess neurotransmitters may in some way predispose the men to violence when they were under stress.

This topic continues on the next spread. ☞

### Essential notes

Studies in this area typically examine whether one particular variant of a candidate gene occurs more often in people who display aggressive behaviour than in a comparison (non-aggressive) group.

### Examiners' notes

When writing about the influence of candidate genes on aggressive behaviour, remember that it is the *gene* that researchers are interested in, as much as the biochemical processes that it controls. Therefore, don't forget to emphasize this in any description.

## Evaluation of genetic factors in aggressive behaviour

### The assumptions of twin studies are not always met

Twin researchers assume that MZ and DZ twins raised in the same environment experience the same environments with their co-twin, therefore any greater similarity between MZ twins must be due to the greater genetic similarity. However, Evans and Martin (2008) suggest that parents, teachers and peers treat MZ twins more similarly than they do DZ twins, therefore greater similarity in terms of aggressive behaviour may also be due to the greater similarity of their experiences.

### Problems with the interpretation of adoption studies

There is an assumption that any similarity between adopted children and their biological parents in terms of aggressive behaviour must be due to genetic factors as they have been raised away from their environmental influence. However, studies in New Zealand and the US (e.g. Fergusson *et al.* 1995) have shown that children given up for adoption display a higher rate of antisocial behaviours (including aggression) compared to the general population *at time of adoption.*

Tremblay (2003) claims that parents who give up their children for adoption also display higher levels of antisocial behaviour compared with adoptive parents. Therefore, the greater similarity in terms of aggression between adopted children and their biological parents may be due *either* to the transmission of antisocial genes from parents to their children or environmental influences (e.g. the parents' antisocial behaviour) prior to adoption.

### Problems of assessing aggression

In the Miles and Carey meta-analysis, the way in which aggression was assessed was a significant moderator of aggressive behaviour reported in the 24 studies. They found that genetic factors explained a larger proportion of the variance in aggression in studies that had used parental or self-reports. However, in studies where aggression was assessed by observational ratings, the contribution of genetic influences was found to be much lower, and environmental factors much higher.

### The role of environmental factors

In the study by Coccaro *et al.*, the researchers found that genetic factors accounted for approximately 40 per cent of the individual differences in aggression. However, they also found that *environmental* influences accounted for 50 per cent of the differences in physical aggression and 70 per cent of the differences in verbal aggression.

In the study by Brunner *et al.*, the finding that violent behaviour was more widespread in the Danish family studied than in 'normal' families, might also be explained in terms of shared environmental factors, such as bad parenting and inappropriate role modelling.

**Examiners' notes**

When answering questions relating to the genetic influences on aggressive behaviour, you need to select material from this spread for your AO2. In A2 questions, marks are given for a balance of breadth and depth, so extensive AO2 points are not always appropriate. On average, you should aim for around 50–60 words for each AO2 point. This degree of elaboration should allow you to demonstrate an appropriate depth and breadth (see p. 39 for more on how to elaborate a point).

## Gene–environment interaction

Rather than genetics or environment alone being responsible for the development of aggressive behaviour, some researchers believe that it is the *interaction* between genetics and environment that determines the likelihood of aggressive behaviour. For example, Caspi *et al.* (2002) discovered a variant of the MAOA gene that was linked with high levels of MAOA and another that was associated with low levels. Those with the variant that was associated with low levels of MAOA were significantly more likely to grow up to exhibit antisocial behaviour but *only* if they had been maltreated as children. Those with the variant that produced high levels of MAOA did not display later antisocial behaviour even if they had been maltreated as children. This supports the claim that it is the *interaction* between genes and aggression that determines the development of aggressive behaviour.

## Issues, debates and approaches

### Genes do not *determine* aggression

Morley and Hall (2003) argue that genes associated with aggression are not **deterministic** and only poorly predict that an individual would display higher levels of aggressive behaviour than the general population. Hines and Malley-Morrison (2005) claim that the finding that aggressive behaviour might be genetically influenced simply means that some people, as a result of their genotype, are *more likely* to commit aggressive acts than are people who do not have the same genotype. In other words, these genetic influences are probabilistic rather than deterministic. Other factors (such as environmental influences) determine whether aggressive behaviour is displayed in a particular situation.

However, some legal experts question the assumption that a violent offender can still exercise free will despite possessing a genetic predisposition to violent crime. For example, in 2009, an Italian judge decided to reduce the prison sentence of a person convicted of murder because he was found to be a carrier of genetic variants thought to be associated with a predisposition to aggressiveness (Forzano *et al.* 2010).

### Real-world application: positive implications of genetics research

Findings from genetics research on antisocial and violent behaviour may have some valuable uses in offender treatment and rehabilitation. Morley and Hall (2003) suggest that information obtained from genetic studies on aggression may be used to help develop interventions for those thought to be at risk of developing criminally violent behaviour. Some scientists and politicians have even advocated genetic engineering as a way of reducing the risk of violent aggression in individuals. However, given the tentative conclusions that can be reached from research in this area, there are considerable ethical consequences of labelling somebody as a 'threat' to society on the basis of their genetic inheritance alone.

# Evolutionary explanations of human aggression

A major concern for our male ancestors was to find a mate, and then having found one, to hold on to her. This need to find and retain a mate brings males into competition with other males. Among early humans, males lived in fear of losing their mate to another male, something that would have devastating consequences for them in terms of passing on their genes to the next generation.

This may well have led to the development of male sexual **jealousy**, a state of fear caused by a real or imagined threat to their status as an exclusive sexual partner. Male sexual jealousy was a consequence of the female's suspected sexual **infidelity** (having sexual relations with other men). Because female sexual infidelity may result in her leaving for a new partner or bearing the child of another man, it had to be deterred at all costs. For our ancestors, sexual jealousy was an **adaptive response**, which has led to the development of adaptive mate-retention behaviours.

## Infidelity and jealousy

### Cuckoldry and jealousy

**Cuckoldry** occurs when a woman deceives her male partner into investing in offspring conceived with another man. Cuckolded men lose both invested resources and reproductive opportunity (Platek and Shackelford 2006). Males have evolved strategies to deter their mates from infidelity and so protect themselves from being cuckolded. According to the evolutionary approach, all such mate-retention strategies are driven by sexual jealousy. Studies of battered women, for example, have shown that the majority of women cite extreme sexual jealousy on the part of their male partners as the key cause of the violence against them (Dobash and Dobash 1984).

### The cuckoldry risk hypothesis (Camilleri 2004)

This predicts that males will be more willing to use sexually coercive tactics such as partner rape when the risk of cuckoldry is high, e.g. when they suspect infidelity or there have been previous instances of infidelity. According to Lalumière *et al.* (2005), some men carry out partner rape in order to decrease paternity uncertainty. Thornhill and Thornhill (1992) argue that a woman who refuses to have sex with her partner may be signalling to him that she has been sexually unfaithful, thus increasing the male's sexual jealousy and fear of cuckoldry.

### Mate retention and violence

Buss and Shackelford (1997) examined mate-retention tactics in married couples. Compared to women, men reported a significantly higher use of intrasexual threats (e.g. threatening to beat up the other man). Women, on the other hand, reported a greater use of verbal possession signals (e.g. indicating to other women than her man 'was taken'). They also found that, men with younger female partners devoted greater effort to mate-retention tactics, including violence against rival males and threats against the female partner.

## Essential notes

**Natural selection** 'weeds out' characteristics that confer no advantage for survival and reproduction, and selects those characteristics that are advantageous. Such characteristics are described as adaptive.

## Examiners' notes

Although infidelity and jealousy are listed in the specification as seemingly separate topics, they are invariably linked in both theory and research, therefore you cannot write about one without also mentioning the other. However, when answering examination questions, you should make the link between them very clear.

## Essential notes

Sexual jealousy evolved as a way of dealing with paternal uncertainty. Because fertilization is internal in human beings, males could never be 100 per cent certain that their offspring are their own.

# The evolution of murder

Buss and Duntley (2006) propose that humans possess adaptations that have evolved specifically through the process of natural selection to produce what we now refer to as 'murder'. According to the evolutionary perspective, murder could not have evolved as a strategy unless it was associated with greater reproductive success than competing strategies. In most circumstances, the extremely high costs of committing murder would have outweighed the benefits of adopting it as a strategy.

Buss and Duntley propose, however, that rare circumstances would have occurred sufficiently often in our evolutionary history where the benefits of murder would have outweighed the costs.

## Murder as an adaptive strategy

Buss and Duntley claim that for our ancestors, murder was functional in solving adaptive problems such as:

- *preventing harm from others* – e.g. through injury or killing of the individual or their family members by other humans
- *reputation management* – e.g. avoiding being perceived as easily exploited or injured by others
- *protecting resources* – e.g. territory, food or mates.

## Predisposing factors for murder

Daly and Wilson (1988) found that men commit the vast majority of murders, and are more likely to kill other men whom they perceive to be sexual rivals or those who challenge their position in the dominance hierarchy. Common predisposing factors include:

- *Sexual jealousy* – Because of the association between infidelity and cuckoldry, men are predominantly the perpetrators and the victims of murder.
- *Lack of resources* – Research on **sexual selection** in humans has shown that females are attracted to males who possess resources. Wilson and Daly (1985) suggest that a lack of resources increases male–male competition and the risk of murder.
- *Threats to male status* – Daly and Wilson argue that females are attracted to males who are dominant over other males and so men are shaped by evolution to seek status. Loss of status would have been catastrophic for our ancestors and so the killing of competitors could have prevented this loss.

**Essential notes**

UK law defines murder as taking a life with 'the intention to kill or do very serious harm'. In the UK, about one in every 100 000 people loses their life to murder.

**Examiners' notes**

You should endeavour, at all times, to make the adaptive nature of murder clear. It is easy to get carried away with florid descriptions of murders and of crime statistics, but it is how and why murder would have evolved that we are interested in here, so this should be explicit in your answer. Remember, also, that even a 24-mark question (25 marks prior to 2012) on evolution and human aggression would only require 200 words (approximately) of AO1 material, and so you could restrict your answer to infidelity and jealousy.

This topic continues on the next spread. ☛

## Evaluation of evolutionary explanations of human aggression

### Supporting evidence for the use of sexual coercion

Research has tended to support the claim that **sexual coercion** of females by their male partners is an adaptive response to the threat of infidelity. Camilleri (2004) found that the risk of a partner's infidelity predicted the likelihood of sexual coercion in men, but not in women. This is significant, because it is men who are at risk of being cuckolded, not women. Goetz and Shackelford (2006) found that women who reported that their partners had sexually coerced them were more likely to admit to having been sexually unfaithful.

### Supporting evidence for mate-retention strategies

Shackelford *et al.* (2005) used a survey method to test predictions concerning the use of mate-retention strategies. Male participants were questioned about their use of mate-retention strategies, and assessed on how often they performed different types of violent acts against their female partners. Consistent with evolutionary predictions, males' use of mate-retention strategies (such as threats) was positively correlated with their violence scores against their mate. In addition, their use of emotional manipulation as a mate-retention strategy (e.g. threatening to kill themselves if their partner left them) also predicted their violence against their partners.

Results from female participants confirmed this trend, with females who reported greater experience of mate-retention strategies from their partners also reporting more incidents of male-initiated violence against them.

### Methodological problems with mate-retention studies

Shackelford and colleagues recognized that the major limitation of their research (and other studies in this area) was that the data was only **correlational**. They were not, therefore, able to establish a causal relationship between the use of mate-retention strategies and violence against women.

An additional problem is the use of the survey method, particularly in such a sensitive area as violence against a partner. The information acquired in this way may not be entirely truthful because of the **social desirability bias** (a tendency to respond in a way that will be viewed favourably by others) thus leading to an underreporting of undesirable behaviour, such as male–female violence.

### The costs of murder from an evolutionary perspective

Although the evolution of murder may be functional for some individuals, the evolution of 'anti-murder' defences would have made this a very risky strategy to pursue. These defences (such as the intended victim killing in self-defence) would make the success rate of murder much lower, as attempting to kill becomes increasingly dangerous for the killer. As a result, natural selection has favoured the development of more covert strategies intended to conceal the killer's intent from their victims in order to avoid activating the anti-murder defences of the other person.

### Limitations of the evolutionary explanation of murder

There is evidence from cross-cultural research that supports the claim that many incidents of male–male killing are a consequence of sexual jealousy. For example, Daly and Wilson found that a common theme was that sexual jealousy was initiated by fairly trivial comments about the sexual attractiveness of another man's wife.

However, Buss and Shackelford claim that an evolutionary perspective on murder cannot explain why people react in different ways when faced with the same adaptive problem. Different men, when confronted with their wife's infidelity, react in very different ways, e.g. with violence (i.e. intersexual aggression) or debasement (i.e. pleading with her not to leave).

## Issues, debates and approaches (IDA)

### Practical applications of research on mate-retention strategies

An important implication of research in this area is that mate-retention strategies may be seen as early indicators of potential violence against a female partner. The use of these strategies can alert family and friends to the danger signs that might lead to future violence in that relationship. Relationship counselling may then be used before the situation escalates into the type of violence reported in the Dobash and Dobash study of battered women (see p. 28).

### Gender bias in studies of mate-retention strategies

Most of the research that has studied infidelity has focused solely on male mate-retention strategies and either male–male or male–female violence. However, females also display mate-retention strategies and can also behave violently towards their male partners (Archer 2000). Archer claims that evidence from family conflict studies shows that women initiate and carry out physical assaults on their partners as often as men. A concentration on males in research therefore gives a gender-biased analysis of the link between jealousy and aggressive behaviour.

### Cultural bias in an evolutionary analysis of aggression

An evolutionary perspective fails to explain why some cultures (e.g. the Yanomamo of South America) seem to *require* male violence to acquire social status, whereas in other cultures (such as the peaceful !Kung San of the Kalahari) aggression leads to irreparable damage to the reputation of the aggressor (Buss and Shackelford). If human aggression (e.g. male–male violence to achieve status) was the consequence of evolved mechanisms, then it would be universal. The fact that cultural differences exist suggests that cultural factors may be more important in the development of human aggression.

### Essential notes

The lack of a universal response to the same adaptive problem casts doubt on the evolutionary perspective being the sole explanation of intersexual aggression. It may, however, suggest a *predisposition* towards intersexual aggression, although the expression of that aggression is determined by many other factors (e.g. previous relationship history, the availability of alternatives, and so on).

### Examiners' notes

You should always remember that *some* IDA content is necessary for a mark in the higher mark bands, so one (or even better, two) of these IDA points should be included in your essay. Remember also that these need to be elaborated in the same way as all the other AO2 points that you may choose to use in response to the question set. See pp. 38–39 for more about IDA and AO2 elaboration.

# Evolutionary explanations of group display in humans

Group behaviour frequently confers advantages on the individuals who make up a particular group. Some behaviours only occur when a collection of like-minded individuals come together for the same purpose. When they join forces and act together, people's behaviour might be regarded as a group display.

## Sports

Fanatical behaviour in sports crowds has a long history: most famously, the riotous fans of the different factions at chariot races during the Roman era. The supporters of two factions in particular, the blues and the greens, were fanatical militants. During the chariot races, politics, religion and sport combined into a dangerously explosive mixture and crowd problems were commonplace.

### Why intergroup aggression?

Among group-living species, natural selection favours genes that cause individual group members to be cooperative with other group members but intolerant toward individuals who are not members of that group (and so could not return any altruistic act). As a result, within the group, **altruism** is promoted and aggression suppressed, whereas between groups, altruism is suppressed and aggression promoted.

In addition, among early humans there was a constant threat from rival groups. Men are hypothesized, therefore, to have evolved a specific tribal psychology that increases their propensity for **intergroup** aggression and includes ingroup favouritism, outgroup derogation (belittling or abuse of outsiders), intergroup aggression and **dehumanization** of the outgroup (van Vugt *et al.* 2007).

### Sports displays and xenophobia

Shaw and Wong (1989) argue that mechanisms that led to suspicion of strangers (**xenophobia**) would have been favoured by natural selection because this would have allowed our ancestors to avoid attack (and harm) and so would have increased their **reproductive fitness**. MacDonald (1992) suggests that it would also be adaptive to exaggerate negative stereotypes of outsiders, as the overperception of threat would be less costly than its underperception.

Evidence for the existence of xenophobia in sports displays was found in Podaliri and Balestri's (1998) analysis of the behaviour of Italian football crowds. They found that the views of extreme right-wing political movements such as the Lega Nord (Northern League) were evident in the chants and banners on Italian football terraces. These displays were openly xenophobic and anti-Semitic. Displays not only expressed outgroup hostility (e.g. between North and South Italian sides) but also served to consolidate ingroup identity and solidarity. For example, in 2009 police arrested 57 *ultras* (football hooligans) from the Sicilian club Catania (a Southern Italian club) who were caught up in a violent clash prior to a match against Atalanta Bergamo (a Northern Italian club).

## Religious group displays

Irons (2001) suggests that a universal dilemma faced by all groups is how to promote cooperation. He argues that throughout human history, the adaptive advantage of group living was the benefits that individuals gained through cooperating with each other (e.g. food sharing, hunting and warfare).

### Credibility enhancing displays

Henrich (2009) suggests a connection between apparently costly group displays (often in ritualized forms such as firewalking, ritual scarification and animal sacrifice) and group solidarity and cooperation. He proposes that humans have evolved to attend to these **credibility enhancing displays (CREDs)**, which provide others with a reliable measure of the individual's actual degree of commitment to a group or belief.

The use of CREDs within a group may arise for many reasons, but their primary function is to signal a deep commitment to the group. Henrich points out that religions with such ritualistic CREDs will tend to survive and grow because these rituals instil a deeper commitment and cooperation than would otherwise be possible. Martyrdom (e.g. in the actions of suicide bombers) can provide powerful CREDs regarding the individual's level of commitment to the group (Atran 2003). The adaptive power of martyrdom is that when others witness this ultimate CRED, it increases the commitment to the cause of the other group members – moderates are likely to become radicals – and the group becomes stronger and more likely to survive.

### Costly signalling to deter free riders

A problem for all groups is how to deal with the 'free rider' – an individual who takes all the advantages of group membership yet fails to cooperate with other group members and gives nothing in return. The significant costs of many religious displays act as a deterrent for anyone who wants to join a group in order to take selfish advantage of the benefits available to group members. Sosis (2006) uses the example of the *Haredim*, ultra-orthodox Jews who wear heavy coats, beards and hats, even in the heat of an Israeli summer. Spending their days in physical discomfort while praying, signals their commitment to the group *and* deters free-riders from taking advantage of the high levels of **intragroup** altruism and cooperation typical of orthodox Jews such as the Haredim.

**Examiners' notes**

When answering exam questions, examples can be used to *elaborate* description (see p. 39), in that they act as evidence to substantiate a particular claim. These examples should be documented rather than mere speculations about what might or might not have happened. For example: the death of insurgent leader Abu Musab al-Zarqawi in an American air strike in 2006 ignited a surge of young male volunteers flowing into Iraq for martyrdom, many of whom would die as suicide bombers (Henrich 2009). This example serves as evidence to extend the claim that martyrdom increases the commitment of other group members.

This topic continues on the next spread. ☞

## Evaluation of evolutionary explanations of group display in humans

### Research support for xenophobia in sports displays

Foldesi (1996) provides support for the link between sports displays and xenophobia in Hungarian football crowds. He found that racist chants and banners from extremist supporters led to an increase in spectator violence in general. Xenophobic abuse was targeted at spectators, players and managers, referees and club officials. Gypsies, Jews and homosexuals were often targets of racist and xenophobic discrimination. Xenophobic abuse was also targeted at Black people and people of other nationalities such as Russians, former Yugoslavians and Romanians.

Evans and Rowe (2002) analysed police reports from 40 football matches played in continental Europe in 1999/2000 involving either English club sides or the English national side. They found more evidence of xenophobic abuse and violent disorder in games involving the national side than in games involving club sides. They interpreted this as due to the fact that club sides tend to be more ethnically diverse and therefore less likely to produce xenophobic responses from foreign supporters.

### An alternative explanation

Marsh's research (Marsh 1978) offers an alternative explanation for the aggressive displays of football crowds that has nothing to do with the adaptive nature of xenophobic displays. He claims that much of the violent behaviour observed on the football terraces is highly ordered and ritualized, and that young working-class males can follow an alternative 'career structure' in football hooliganism.

### Research support for costly religious displays

Sosis and Bressler (2003) provide support for the claim that more costly displays of religious commitment (e.g. CREDs) are an important determinant of the success of religious groups. They found that religious groups imposed far more costly requirements on their members than secular (i.e. non-religious) groups. The magnitude of these costly requirements was also positively correlated with the lifespan of the group. This supports the claim that religions that require the greatest displays of commitment produce the most committed members and so last the longest.

A further claim is that costly displays deter free-riders from taking selfish advantage of the benefits offered by group membership. Chen (2003) found that, during the Indonesian financial crisis in the 1990s, Muslim families donated a significant proportion of their financial resources to religious observance. Chen concluded that in times of crisis, religious groups provide a form of social insurance for needy individuals within the group, supporting the idea that in close-knit communities, cooperation confers benefits to group members.

---

**Examiners' notes**

In order to include an alternative explanation as part of your AO2 evaluation, you should offer some comment on why your alternative explanation is a better explanation of the facts than the one being evaluated. In this case, Marsh's research might better explain why xenophobic and racist displays are more common among young working-class male football supporters, because his explanation (football violence as a career structure) sees this behaviour as a way in which disempowered young males can achieve social status.

## Cultural factors in the type of display

Sosis *et al.* (2005) collected data from 60 geographically dispersed societies on the costs of group rituals and the frequency of warfare. They found that the frequency of warfare was the strongest predictor of the costliness of that society's male ritual displays. They also found that the nature of warfare (i.e. internal, within the society, or external, with other societies) was related to the type of display favoured by males.

- Sosis and colleagues found a positive correlation between permanent displays of group membership (such as ritual body scars) and external warfare.

- In societies where internal warfare was the norm, and group membership was liable to change, displays tended to be more temporary (e.g. body painting).

This supports the claim that costly male ritualistic displays have evolved to signal commitment and promote solidarity among males who must cooperate in warfare.

## Issues, debates and approaches (IDA)

### Real-world application

The rise in xenophobic displays among football supporters has led football clubs to take steps to minimize their influence. Club-based antiracism initiatives have included football clinics and coaching courses for minorities, and taking measures to eliminate racism within the ground.

In Scotland, the sectarian displays commonly observed amongst the fans of Rangers (a Protestant club) and Celtic (a Catholic club) have been addressed by the two Glasgow clubs. Celtic have initiated the 'Bhoys Against Bigotry' campaign, cracking down on xenophobic bigotry within Celtic Park. The singing of IRA songs, for example, has been forbidden on the terraces. Rangers finally abandoned their long-standing tradition against the signing of Catholic players.

### An evolutionary approach

Understanding the adaptive value of religious displays allows us to explain the success of different religions from a purely evolutionary perspective. However, this perspective would also suggest that, although *intragroup* solidarity is a significant adaptive advantage, a disadvantage is that this accentuates *intergroup* conflict. This appears to be the case, in that societies with more costly religious displays tend to experience higher levels of intergroup conflict (Roes and Raymond 2003).

The Nuer people in Ethiopia practise ritual scarification and boys typically get these horizontal scars across their forehead.

**Examiners' notes**

In order to develop some of the ideas on these two pages, you could try to research your own support to make your material more personal and therefore more meaningful. For example: does membership of religious groups confer benefits to its members? And is there a relationship between the magnitude of benefits offered and the costs (e.g. of ritualistic displays or religious observance) expected of its members?

# Answering A2 examination questions

## AO1, AO2 and AO3

The A2 examination assesses three 'assessment objectives' known as AO1, AO2 and AO3:

- **AO1** assesses your ability to recall and show your understanding of scientific knowledge – e.g. describing a theory or study.
- **AO2** assesses your ability to analyse and evaluate scientific knowledge – e.g. evaluating a theory in terms of research support.
- **AO3** is concerned with 'How Science Works' – e.g. methodological criticisms of research studies.

## Be prepared

A2 questions will often occur as parted questions and these different parts can also occur with different mark allocations. For example, question (a) on a particular topic could be worth:

- 4, 5 or 9 marks (for exams up to 2011), or
- 4 or 8 marks (for exams from 2012 onwards).

This means that not only should you be aware of all the topics on which you may be questioned, but you should also have practised examination type answers for these to fit the varying mark allocations.

For example, if you have covered the Unit 3 topic of aggression and included deindividuation theory as one of your social psychological theories of aggression, then you should be able to produce a 'shorter version' outline of the theory to answer a shorter 4- or 5-mark question, as well as being able to produce a 'longer version' outline of the explanation for an 8- or 9-mark question. This has two clear benefits:

- You will have the information you need to produce enough descriptive material for a higher mark allocation question.
- You won't waste valuable exam time by overproducing an answer for a smaller mark allocation.

## Use your time wisely

Examinations are held under time constraints, and so you must use your time wisely. Students often waste far too much time doing things that are not required, e.g. stating *'In this essay I am going to…'* or providing irrelevant information. This means that they don't have sufficient time to do the things they *should* be doing, and so lose many of the marks available.

## Read for understanding

When reading a question, ensure that you fully understand its requirements. Far too often, students focus in on a certain word or phrase that identifies the particular topic being examined and base their answer solely on that. After expending much time and effort, they then realize that they are not answering the question as it should be answered or discover

**Examiners' notes**

On this paper, AO1 is worth 9 marks (8 marks from 2012) of every question, and AO2/AO3 is worth 16 marks of every question. This is very important, as it should inform the way you structure your response to exam questions.

**Examiners' notes**

At AS level, there are distinct questions (and mark allocations) for AO3, but at A2 level this is not the case, and AO3 is simply part of your AO2 mark allocation (referred to as AO2/AO3). This is justified because in evaluating theories and/or research studies, you will invariably include some of the research evidence, ethical issues, reliability, validity, etc., that constitute AO3.

they cannot answer the question as well as they first imagined. Therefore, make sure you have read the entire question and fully understand its requirements *before* starting to answer it.

## Make a plan

When you have fully understood the question and have decided that you are able to answer it, then it's also a good idea to prepare a small plan of points to be made, possibly in bullet point form numbered in a logical order. This not only gives you a plan to follow, but also protects against forgetting some of these points mid-answer. It also helps you to engage with the material, which again is a useful strategy towards producing higher-quality answers.

## Effective evaluation

Students can often become confused, especially under exam conditions, as to what to include in an answer requiring evaluation. A good way to combat this problem is to include the 'recipe' method as a regular part of your revision. Thus, when planning the evaluative content for an answer, list all the different elements that could comprise evaluation. This will vary slightly from question to question depending on the wording, but generally you should have:

- examples of research that both supports and weakens points being made
- practical applications
- IDA points (see below)
- methodological points (especially in questions specifically about research studies)
- implications
- theoretical support.

You may not actually use all of this material, but you should produce answers with good breadth of evaluation, as well as reducing the chances of having insufficient material or of using non-creditworthy material.

## Issues, debates and approaches (IDA)

An important feature of the AO2 marking allocation is that examiners look for evidence of issues, debates or approaches in your answer. There are many different ways of addressing this requirement, including the following:

- *issues* – gender and cultural bias, ethical issues, real world application
- *debates* – psychology as science, reductionism, free-will/determinism, nature/nurture
- *approaches* – biological, evolutionary, psychodynamic, etc.

Opportunities for IDA are flagged up throughout this book, so it is a good idea to practise generating these for all the topics relevant to A2 aggression.

## Elaboration in AO2 evaluation

AO2 assesses your ability to analyse and evaluate scientific knowledge relevant to a specific topic area. When allocating marks for AO2 questions, examiners look for appropriateness and elaboration. One way of *elaborating* effectively is to use the 'three-point rule'. This involves:

- *identifying* the critical point
- *justifying* it
- *explaining* why this is good (or bad) for the theory or explanation being evaluated.

For example, if your criticism is that a study lacks ecological validity, this point can be elaborated thus:

> 'This study lacks validity (*identification*), because research by X failed to replicate the findings of Y (*justification*), which therefore means that the findings of Y's research cannot be generalized beyond the specific situation of that experiment (*explanation*)'.

**Examiners' notes**

In 2012, the number of marks allocated for AO1 will be 8 (down from 9), whereas the number of marks available for AO2/AO3 will stay the same at 16 marks.

## Using the right terminology

As well as having a good understanding of psychological concepts and topics, you also need to be able to communicate your understanding to others. A useful and simple means of achieving this is by using psychological terminology wherever relevant in exam answers. Try to develop a good working knowledge of psychological terminology throughout your studies – and practise using it – in order to become proficient in this skill. However, be careful not to use jargon for its own sake, as this can lead to the danger of writing incomprehensible answers that appear muddled.

## Example questions and answers with examiner comments

On the following pages you will find sample questions followed by sample average and strong answers, and also tinted boxes containing the comments and advice of the examiners. Answers refer to content within the revision section of this book and additional content, providing you with the opportunity to consolidate and extend your revision and research.

# AQA Unit 3 Topics in Psychology: Aggression

## Example Paper 1

### Question 1

*Discuss **two or more** social psychological theories of aggression.*
**[25 marks** (2009 onwards)] **[24 marks** (2012 onwards)]

This question has a number of distinct requirements:
- The use of a command word such as 'Discuss' indicates that both AO1 (description) and AO2 (evaluation) are required. Although it is not made explicit in the question, the 25 marks (24 marks 2012 onwards) are divided into 9 marks (8 marks 2012 onwards) for description and 16 marks for evaluation. This equates to about one-third description and two-thirds evaluation.
- All questions on the Unit 3 paper require some content that covers 'Issues, debates and approaches' (IDA). There is no need to provide all three, but failure to provide at least one will lead to a restricted mark for AO2.

- The instruction 'two or more' indicates that more than one theory is required. Answers restricted to just one theory would not be able to receive all the marks available. It is up to you to choose which theories you write about. The most obvious ones would be social learning theory and deindividuation. If you choose the 'or more' option (i.e. write about three or even four theories), there is a danger of your explanations being too superficial – in this case, more explanations do not necessarily lead to more marks.
- Finally, beware of including theories that are not social psychological in nature (e.g. evolutionary or biological). They simply would not attract marks.

**Average answer**

In this essay I will describe the social learning theory of aggression and the deindividuation theory. I will then evaluate both theories.

The social learning theory was first described by Albert Bandura. He carried out the Bobo doll studies. Children watched an adult beating up an inflatable doll. The children were then frustrated by being allowed to see some attractive toys but not being allowed to play with them. When the children were let into the room with the Bobo doll, they hit the doll in the same way and shouted the same insults. This led Bandura to conclude that children learned aggression by observing others and then imitating the behaviours they had observed. A problem with this research is that the children were only hitting a doll not a real person – therefore the experiment lacks mundane reality. In a follow-up to this experiment, children watched a model being either rewarded for their aggression or punished by another adult. Children who saw the model being rewarded were more likely to imitate their aggressive behaviour than children who saw the model being punished. ☞

This paragraph is largely a waste of space. Detailing intentions does not help to answer the specific question set.

Giving too much description, as here, is a common mistake that students make when answering questions on this particular area. The question asks for theories not studies; the answer should focus more on what the Bobo doll studies have contributed to our understanding of aggression – not just describe the study itself.

The student goes on to evaluates the study rather than the theory ('A problem with this research…'), and so the evaluation is of limited relevance.

The final two sentences contain relevant description and do a better job of detailing one of the important characteristics of the social learning theory explanation of aggression.

An advantage of this explanation is that it can explain how children can be affected by watching violence on TV. Research has shown how, if children observe aggressive models on television, particularly if they see them being rewarded for their aggression (e.g. a bully), they are more likely to imitate their aggression in their own behaviour.

This is better: the evaluative point being made is relevant and elaborated. The fact that the connection between media violence and real-life imitation is not clear does not detract from the point being made.

Social learning theory is related to cognitive psychology because children must form a mental representation of the behaviour, together with an expectation of whether aggressive behaviour would be likely to be rewarded or punished in the future.

Linking social learning theory to cognitive psychology could count towards the 'Issues, debates and approaches' (IDA) requirement of the question.

Deindividuation theory was first formulated by Zimbardo in his Stanford Prison Experiment. He found that when students dressed as prison guards or prisoners, they became deindividuated and the guards acted aggressively towards the prisoners. Zimbardo also carried out a study where students had to give electric shocks to other students when they were either in a deindividuated state or in an individuated state. They were more likely to deliver the shocks when they were in the deindividuated state.

This paragraph is not particularly effective as it never actually tells us what deindividuation is. It also doesn't explain how participants in the experiments *became* deindividuated or why deindividuation might be associated with increased aggression.

Deindividuation is also likely when people are in large crowds. An application of this theory is that it can be used to explain the strange behaviour of the baiting crowd, when people in a large crowd are more likely to encourage suicide jumpers to jump. It has also been used to explain the behaviour of lynch mobs. Research has shown the bigger the mob, the more ferocious they were.

This could also count as part of the IDA requirement of the question. However, it isn't used that effectively other than to point out that as mobs get larger, they are more likely to be violent. What *other* aspects of their behaviour (e.g. darkness, distance from victim) could support the idea of deindividuation being responsible?

An anthropologist, Robert Watson looked at different tribes and found that those tribes that dressed up and wore war paint were more likely to kill and mutilate their victims than tribes that didn't.

Here, good material is introduced but the student fails to do much with it. To turn it into a useful AO2 point, the student needs to point out *which* aspects of deindividuation theory this supports.

There have been suggestions that deindividuation could explain football crowd violence, but this has been criticized because much of the violence found among football crowds is more ritualized (e.g. chants) than physical, and in many cases, the violence is carefully organized rather than being the result of deindividuation.

This could also count as IDA as it is an application, and this time the elaboration is more effective.

Deindividuation has been criticized by Deiner who found evidence that when people were in a deindividuated state they were just as likely to act in a prosocial way. Zimbardo's prison study can also be criticized. Zimbardo claimed that under conditions where people were deindividuated they would be more likely to commit violent acts, and he used Abu Ghraib as an example. However, Haslam and Reicher argue that violent behaviour when anonymous is a choice rather than being determined.

The AO2 point in the first sentence is appropriate, but isn't really elaborated. What is the evidence to support Deiner's criticism?

The paragraph goes on to make a decent evaluative point, and there is some elaboration (e.g. the reference to Abu Ghraib and Haslam and Reicher's counter claim).

**Average answer: overall comment**

This student has not really thought too much about the mark split, so has probably included as much AO1 material as AO2 material instead of one-third AO1 to two-thirds AO2.

- AO1 – The AO1 material is reasonable, although it lacks depth at times, and perhaps the Bobo doll studies have masked a real description of social learning theory. The answer doesn't state explicitly what deindividuation is, nor the conditions that foster it. To get high marks, an answer should include a very clear exposition of the main claims of the theories being described, rather than forcing the examiner to pick through implied references to theoretical points, as in this essay.

- AO2 – Some decent points are made, but these are not always elaborated, so this is somewhere between 'basic' and 'reasonable' for the AO2 marks.

It would not take much to push the marks up closer to the A grade answers – mostly what is needed is clear and appropriate elaboration of the critical points being made. However, as it stands, this would be worth a Grade C.

**Strong answer**

Social learning theory proposes that children learn to be aggressive by observing the behaviour of role models. When they observe these role models being rewarded for their aggressive behaviour, they are motivated to imitate the aggressive behaviour they have witnessed in order to receive the same rewards. This is known as vicarious reinforcement.

Bandura claimed that as part of the social learning process, children must form a mental representation of the behaviour they have observed as well as any rewards or punishments that are associated with it. Social learning theorists believe that by watching others, either in real life or on television, children learn scripts that later guide their own behaviour. When the child is subsequently in a similar situation, they will be able to reproduce the same form of aggressive behaviour, provided the expectation of receiving a reward is greater than the expectation of being punished for being aggressive.

Social learning theory is able to explain why people may be aggressive in one situation, but not in another. This is because aggression may be reinforced (or seen to be reinforced) in some situations, but not in others; therefore, the person is motivated to be aggressive in some situations but not in others. This supports the main claims of social learning theory, that people learn not only how to perform aggressive behaviours, but also whether they are appropriate in a particular situation.

Social learning theory was based on Bandura's studies using a Bobo doll. A problem with this theory is that there are ethical issues associated with exposing children to violent behaviour in studies such as this. As a result, studies such as Bandura's Bobo doll study would no longer be allowed. This makes the social learning theory difficult to test among children.

There are methodological problems with these studies, particularly because a Bobo doll is not a living thing and does not respond when hit in the way that a human being might. However, Bandura also used a film of an adult hitting a live clown. Children who watched this film later imitated the aggressive behaviours they had seen in the film. ☞

This is how an essay of this sort *should* start, straight into a description of the first theory rather than wasting time with stating intentions (i.e. 'In this essay I will…') or needless definitions (e.g. 'Aggression is defined as…').

Higher marks are earned for descriptions that are *detailed* as this one is here.

Starting a new paragraph is a good way of dividing material to ensure the right balance of AO1 and AO2. This following section is carefully constructed so it is entirely AO2. The use of phrases such as 'This supports the main claims of…' emphasizes that this is AO2 material and suggests to the examiner that the student understands the significance of this particular point as part of a critical argument.

The point that there are ethical issues with the Bobo doll studies helps to fulfil the IDA requirement of the question. As with other points, it is important that this is sufficiently detailed to warrant a mark in the higher mark bands.

Citing methodological problems with the underlying research counts as AO3 material (see p. 37). This is accurate and appropriately detailed.

A second explanation is deindividuation theory. When people are in an individuated state, aggressive behaviour is inhibited because of the need to behave in a socially acceptable manner. In some situations, such as submerged in the anonymity of a large crowd, these inhibitions become relaxed. As a result, people in a deindividuated state are more likely to act aggressively. Zimbardo (1969) demonstrated deindividuation in a lab experiment. He put participants in either an individuated condition or a deindividuated condition, and required them to deliver electric shocks to another participant. He found that participants in the deindividuated condition delivered shocks for twice as long as did those in the individuated condition.

Johnson and Downing (1979) repeated the Zimbardo study, but had participants in one group wear masks and overalls and in the other group wear nurses' uniforms. Participants shocked more than the control group when dressed in mask and overalls, but less than the control group when dressed like nurses. This challenges the claim that deindividuation always leads to aggressive behaviour and suggests that people respond to the different norms of the situation they find themselves in.

Although some research has supported the claims of deindividuation theory, other studies have challenged it. A meta-analysis of deindividuation studies (Postmes and Spears 1998) found insufficient support for the claim that antisocial aggressive behaviour is more common in large groups or in anonymous settings.

Research suggests gender differences in the effects of deindividuation. Cannavale et al. (1970) found that males were more likely to behave aggressively under conditions of deindividuation, but females were not. This suggests that males are more prone to losing their inhibitions about aggressive behaviour when in a deindividuated state than are females. Because of these differences, it suggests that research carried out solely on males (or females) would not tell us how deindividuation affects the other sex, thus indicating a gender bias.

It is a good idea to indicate clearly what the second explanation is, as this student does. This also makes it clear where one explanation ends and the next one begins. Studies can be used either as AO1 or (when built into a critical argument) as AO2. Here it is being used as AO1 description as it elaborates the description of deindividuation.

It would be easy to put too much descriptive detail into this study, particularly when it is being used to make an evaluative point, but this is just about right.

The final sentence is vital to turn it into a clearly evaluative one. It demonstrates the significance of Johnson and Downing's study as part of the evaluation of deindividuation theory.

This is effective use of supporting evidence, particularly as it indicates the particular claim of the theory that it challenges, rather than just saying it challenges the theory as a whole.

Gender differences count as part of the IDA requirement of the question. Here, this is built into a critical argument effectively rather than just pointing out that there are gender differences in deindividuation. The student clarifies the importance of this gender difference by pointing out how this could constitute a gender bias in our interpretation of deindividuation research findings.

**Strong answer: overall comment**

A striking feature of this essay is how carefully and deliberately it has been laid out. The AO1 description and the AO2 evaluation are in distinct paragraphs, and this also tells us that the overall balance of the essay is almost exactly right for the mark split between AO1 and AO2.

- AO1 – Theories are described clearly and accurately, and the student has avoided covering too many theories and so making the answer superficial.

- AO2 – Analysis and evaluation are appropriate, and are elaborated carefully for maximum impact, while issues, debates and approaches (IDA) are included as a clear part of the overall evaluation.

Overall, this answer is clearly Grade A quality.

## Question 2

### Part (a)

*Outline the role of genetic factors in aggressive behaviour.* [**4 marks**]

There are a number of points to note about this part of question 2:
- Only 4 marks are available and this might catch some students unawares. You would expect to write about 100 to 120 words for a 4-mark question.

- The marks are all AO1, requiring descriptive material only, in the form of a brief outline of how genetic factors have been shown to influence aggression – e.g. a précis of the findings of research into twin and/or adoption studies.
- It is important to ensure that all material included is *explicitly* linked to genetic factors.

### Average answer

There have been a number of twin studies that have shown that identical twins are more similar in terms of aggression than are non-identical twins. For example, one study found that identical twins were 75% concordant for aggression whereas non-identical twins were only 35% concordant. Other studies have also found a large genetic component in aggression. For example, a meta-analysis carried out in 2002 found that 50% of aggressive behaviour was inherited.

The student has some accuracy, but also some vagueness and some inaccuracy. They are right that MZ twins are more alike in terms of accuracy, but wrong with their detail of 75 per cent/35 per cent. They don't name the 2002 meta-analysis (likely to be Rhee and Waldman), which actually found a figure of 40 per cent heritability, but if we ignore the date, another large meta-analysis (Miles and Carey) did estimate 50 per cent heritability. This answer would score about half of the four marks available.

### Strong answer

Both twin and adoption studies have shown an important role for genetic factors in aggression. For example, a twin study by Coccaro *et al.* (1997) found that genes accounted for more than 40% of the individual differences in aggressive behaviour. An adoption study by Hutchings and Mednick (1973) found a significant positive correlation between convictions for criminal violence between biological fathers and their adopted sons, suggesting that these genetic influences persist despite the lack of a shared environment.
Finally, a meta-analysis of 51 twin and adoption studies (Rhee and Waldman 2002) estimated that the genetic component in antisocial behaviour was approximately 40%.

This is a well-informed, detailed and *accurate* summary of research in this area. The student has fleshed out their answer with appropriate detail, and altogether this gives an accurate and entirely appropriate snapshot of the link between genetics and aggression. This answer would be worth the full four marks available for this part of the question.

## Part (b)

*Outline and evaluate evolutionary explanations of infidelity **and/or** jealousy.*
**[5 + 16 marks** (2009 onwards)] **[4 + 16 marks** (2012 onwards)]

- When a question is in parts and has both AO1 and AO2 marks, the split will be indicated, as here. This will dictate how much descriptive material (AO1) and how much evaluative material (AO2) you provide in response. This is another disaster waiting to happen for the unaware student, who might be tempted to present equal amounts of AO1 description and AO2 evaluation. With a 5/16 mark split, this means writing about one-quarter AO1 and three-quarters AO2. For exams from 2012, the mark split is 4/16, which means writing just one-fifth AO1 and two-fifths AO2. This is vital, because an examiner has separate mark bands for AO1 and AO2 and can't award more than the marks specified for each.

- Part (b) also gives an **and/or** choice (i.e. infidelity and/or jealousy). This is partly because they are conceptually linked, as sexual jealousy tends to be a consequence of suspected infidelity. It is difficult to write about one without also mentioning the other, so most answers would include reference to both (although this is not a requirement of the question).

### Average answer

Infidelity is when one partner has sex with someone outside the marriage. If it is the woman who has sex with someone else, there is the possibility that her husband will end up raising a child that is not his own. This is called cuckoldry. Men can never be certain that a child is their own, because fertilization takes place out of sight. The possibility of cuckoldry makes men experience sexual jealousy, which is an adaptive response designed to prevent the female from having sex with other men. As a result of men experiencing sexual jealousy, men may behave more aggressively toward their partner. This form of aggression is called mate-guarding, and men have evolved a number of mate-guarding strategies to try and stop their mates from committing infidelity. One of these strategies is to use threats of violence or to give presents so that their partners think twice about straying. Another, more extreme form of mate-retention strategies is to use sexual violence against their partner, i.e. by raping them. Raping the partner may decrease the chance of her becoming pregnant by another man and so lower the chance of cuckoldry.

There is research to support many of these claims. For example, Buss and Shackelford carried out a study in 1997 where they interviewed men and woman and asked them questions about whether they had ever used or experienced mate-retention strategies. They found that men were much more likely than women to have ☞

This paragraph is all description, but the student has made the mistake of putting too much detail in (it is only worth five marks after all). The material is certainly appropriate, but the time spent writing it will be at the expense of the AO2 material that is worth almost three times as many marks for this part of the question.

The Buss and Shackelford study is used well (e.g. the student has introduced it by the AO2 phrase 'There is research to support...'). However, the additional finding of this study is merely introduced by the assertion that it is 'interesting', and we are not told why this finding is significant. The final sentence would count as IDA content, but it is fairly brief and appears almost as an afterthought.

used threats against their partner (e.g. threatening to beat up the man they suspected to be having an affair with their wife). They also found something very interesting, that men were more likely to experience sexual jealousy and to use mate-retention strategies when they were married to a younger woman. The other evidence to support the link between sexual jealousy and aggression comes from studies of woman in a battered wives' refuge. The women in these refuges frequently report sexual jealousy as the main reason that their husbands had behaved aggressively against them. In fact, in one study, it was found that three-quarters of the women who reported the use of this sort of mate-retention strategy by their husbands had needed medical attention as a result. There is an important application of this research that shows the use of mate-retention strategies, because it means that relationship counselling can be initiated by the female (or by the male) before it escalates into violence and injury for the wife.

**Average answer: overall comment**

The answer is let down by part (b), where the imbalance of the content holds back the overall grade to a Grade C band answer.

**Strong answer**

Daly and Wilson claim that men have evolved a number of mate-retention strategies to deter their partners from committing infidelity with another man. The dangers associated with this are that the man ends up wasting his resources on another man's child (cuckoldry). The adaptation that helps men to deal with this possibility is sexual jealousy. According to the evolutionary approach, male retention strategies are driven by sexual jealousy. These strategies include sexual coercion, forcing an unwilling partner into having sex in order to minimize parental uncertainty and so reduce the risk of cuckoldry, intersexual violence (physical aggression or threats of physical aggression against partners who have been, or are suspected of being, unfaithful) and violence against intrasexual rivals.

Research by Camilleri (2004) provided support for the claim that males are likely to use sexual coercion when they suspect infidelity on the part of the female partner. This was not the case when women suspected male infidelity, which makes sense as only males are at risk of cuckoldry. Buss and Shackelford (1997) provide further research evidence to support these gender differences. They found that men reported a greater use of threats against their partner (or the other male) when they suspected infidelity than did women. They also found that the use of mate-retention strategies such as threatening violence was more likely when the female was younger (i.e. a 'higher value mate') because the risk of cuckoldry was greater with such females. Shackelford et al. (2005) provided survey evidence to show that the use of mate-retention strategies such as threats of aggression was positively related to actual violence against the female. This claim was supported by male reports of their own use of these strategies, and also by female reports of their own experience of threats and intersexual violence. However, the validity of survey data may be suspect when used in sensitive areas such as violence against a spouse. For some individuals, answers may not be completely truthful because of the social desirability bias. Other evidence for the use of intersexual violence comes from studies of battered wives.

This is a proper length for an entirely AO1 paragraph and shows an appropriate selection of material, presented accurately and in detail. It is focused on the link between infidelity, sexual jealousy and aggression throughout. A very effective AO1 paragraph.

Dobash and Dobash (1984) found that victims frequently cited extreme sexual jealousy as the primary reason for the violence against them. There is, however, a gender bias in research on infidelity as most studies have focused on mate-retention behaviours in males, and male violence against females. Evidence from family conflict studies suggests that there are approximately equal amounts of intersexual violence initiated by males and females (Archer 2000). Family conflict studies have also led to an important application of research. Mate-retention strategies may be seen as an 'early-warning' system for possible violence against a partner. Evidence of mate-retention strategies can alert family and friends so that intervention, such as relationship counselling, may be offered before the situation escalates into actual violence against the partner. This is a real social problem, as Wilson et al. (1995) reported that among women who reported experiencing direct-guarding by their partner as a mate-retention strategy, 72% required medical treatment following an assault by their partner.

Both of these latter paragraphs are entirely AO2 evaluation. The material is carefully constructed into an evaluative argument, and each point is elaborated. For example, the Shackelford et al. study is not just described (in which case it would just be more AO1), but it is made into AO2 by an appropriate linking phrase ('provided survey evidence to show that …') and further elaboration in terms of the limitations of survey data. The material is accurate and shows an excellent understanding of the area. Two good IDA points close out the essay, one on gender bias that goes beyond mere assertion, and the other how research has led to a valuable social application.

**Strong answer: overall comment**

This is a high-quality, very well balanced essay, which would certainly be worth a high Grade A.

## Question 3

*Discuss the role of neural **and** hormonal mechanisms in aggression.*
**[25 marks** (2009 onwards)] **[24 marks** (2012 onwards)]

There are several points to note about this question:
- As with question 1, the use of the command term 'Discuss' indicates a need for both AO1 and AO2 material, weighted more towards AO2 – see next point.
- With questions that just indicate 25 marks available (24 marks 2012 onwards), there are just 9 marks (8 marks 2012 onwards) out of 25 available for AO1 (description) and 16 out of 25 for AO2 (evaluation). That means that two-thirds of your material should be AO2.

- The question specifies both neural and hormonal mechanisms, so answers that included only one would be penalized. Although the term 'mechanisms' is plural, that does *not* mean you have to write about more than one 'mechanism' for each area, although if only one mechanism per area was included, the answer might lack breadth and be seen as fairly limited. Likely material would include the role of serotonin and dopamine (neural mechanisms), and testosterone and cortisol (hormonal mechanisms).

**Average answer**

In this essay I will begin by describing the role played by neural mechanisms in aggression. These are neurotransmitters, which are chemicals in the brain that carry signals across the synapse. I will look at research that has been carried out on the role of neurotransmitters in aggression and then try to evaluate that research and the role of neural mechanisms generally. I will then look at the role of hormonal mechanisms in aggression. Hormones are produced by glands in the endocrine system and are carried in the bloodstream to have an action in another part of the body. It is believed that one of the actions that they have is on aggressive behaviour. I will review research evidence on the role of hormones on aggression and then evaluate this research and the role of hormonal mechanisms generally.

The most important neurotransmitter involved in aggression is serotonin. Low levels of serotonin in the brain are thought to be associated with aggressive behaviour. We know this because there are low levels of waste products of serotonin in people who have high levels of aggressive behaviour. The other important neurotransmitter is dopamine. Increases in dopamine are thought to be associated with high levels of aggression. We know this because drugs that block dopamine in the brain have been shown to reduce aggressive behaviour. ☞

This is an entirely wasted opening paragraph, yet is very common in exam answers. Students are often told to tell the reader what they intend to do in an essay, but this simply isn't appropriate in an exam essay, where you have just 30 minutes to carry out the explicit requirements of the question. Take heed and don't waste time!

Support for the importance of serotonin comes from studies that have used a chemical to reduce the amount of serotonin in the brain. In one study carried out by Mann *et al.* in 1990, a drug was given that reduced serotonin levels, and then participants were given a questionnaire to fill in. They found that hostility and aggression were highest in those people who had been given the serotonin-reducing drug. An alternative explanation for the low serotonin explanation is that aggressive people don't metabolize serotonin properly. The influence of serotonin may possibly explain why alcohol is associated with aggressive behaviour because alcohol is known to reduce serotonin levels and thus increase aggression. The role of dopamine in aggressive behaviour is supported by research with rats. Ferrari *et al.* allowed a rat to fight every day for 11 days, but on the 12th day, the rat wasn't allowed to fight and the researchers measured its dopamine and serotonin levels instead. They found that the rat had high levels of dopamine and low levels of serotonin, which is what was predicted to be the case.

The hormone that is most associated with aggression is testosterone. High levels of testosterone are thought to be associated with aggressive behaviour. We know this because of research that looked at levels of testosterone in delinquent boys and found them to be higher than in non-delinquent boys. Evidence also comes from animal studies that have found that when animals have their testosterone levels increased, this produces an increase in aggression. The problem with the testosterone aggression link is that the evidence tends to be inconsistent, with some studies showing very little evidence between the two. There are also some positive effects of testosterone, as research has shown that testosterone therapy can raise mood in many older people.

This evaluation is appropriate but lacks the elaboration that we might expect in a high-grade answer. For example, the 'faulty metabolism' explanation is offered as an alternative, yet nothing is done with this information, so it fails to have much impact. Similarly, the alcohol/serotonin/aggression link is interesting, but would have been more effective if some evidence were present to substantiate the claim. There is a slight inaccuracy in the answer as it should be '... for 10 days, but on the 11th day', rather than '... for 11 days, but on the 12th day', but this is not important and does not impact on the mark awarded.

The final paragraph is a rather superficial treatment of hormonal mechanisms. There is a clear need for some research evidence, which might have been used to add detail to the descriptive component and also to add research support as evaluation. Although there is no need for the two halves of the answer (neural and hormonal) to be of equal length, they should be better balanced than here.

**Average answer: overall comment**

This answer loses marks because of the wasted first paragraph, a lack of detail and elaboration, and an imbalance between neural and hormonal mechanisms.

There is lots of potential for a higher-grade answer, but as it stands, this is around Grade C/D standard.

**Strong answer**

Aggression in humans has been associated with low levels of serotonin and high levels of dopamine. Usually, serotonin has a calming effect, which inhibits aggression. When levels of serotonin are low, this inhibitory effect is removed and people are less able to control their aggressive behaviour. Evidence for the importance of serotonin comes from two main sources. First, Brown et al. (1982) found that there were low levels of the waste products of serotonin in the cerebrospinal fluid of individuals who are prone to impulsive and aggressive behaviour. The second source of evidence is studies where participants were given the drug dexfenfluramine, which reduces levels of serotonin in the brain. Mann et al. (1990) administered dexfenfluramine to male and female participants, and found that males (but not females) displayed more aggressive responses on a questionnaire.

A meta-analysis of 29 studies of serotonin and aggression showed that these studies consistently found evidence of low serotonin levels in antisocial children and adults. The levels of serotonin were particularly low in individuals who had attempted suicide, suggesting that low levels of serotonin lead to impulsive behaviour, one consequence of which is aggressive behaviour and, in some individuals, suicide. One of the consequences of low levels of serotonin is that the brain creates more receptors in an attempt to capture any serotonin that is available. This has been shown to be the case in research by Arora and Meltzer (1989), who found elevated levels of serotonin receptors in people who had committed violent suicide, thus supporting the claim that normal levels of serotonin have an inhibitory influence on violent behaviour. Ferrari et al. (2003) showed support for serotonin in aggressive behaviour in an animal study of rats. They allowed rats to fight at the same time every day for 10 days, and then not on the 11th day. They found that the rats learned from their experience and had raised levels of serotonin in anticipation of having to fight. Serotonin explanations of aggression have been criticized as being reductionist. The link between serotonin and aggression is fairly well established in non-human animals, but the position is less clear in humans, particularly as aggressive behaviour in humans is a far more complex behaviour, and is subject to social learning, genetics, etc. ☞

An excellent opening paragraph, which is entirely descriptive, although arguably the evidence might be used as evaluation. However, examiners do have the discretion to choose whether something like this would best serve the student as AO1 or AO2, and in this case, given the high quality of the AO2 that follows, it would probably be credited as AO1.

This is very competent and well-informed AO2. The impressive characteristic about this paragraph is that the material chosen is all used effectively to construct a thorough critical examination of the role of serotonin. It finishes with a good explanation of the reductionist argument, which goes beyond merely asserting that the explanation is reductionist and offers reasons why this is the case. There is no mention of dopamine, but there is no need for this as discussion of serotonin is perfectly adequate as a demonstration of neural mechanisms in aggressive behaviour.

Testosterone has been associated with aggressive behaviour, although most studies have been correlational only – for example, a meta-analysis by Archer (1991) found a low positive correlation between testosterone levels and aggression. A study by Kouri et al. (1995), gave participants either testosterone or a placebo. They were then told that, by pressing a button they could reduce the amount of cash that another participant was receiving. Those who received the testosterone pressed the button more than those with the placebo. An advantage of this study is that it made use of the experimental method, so allowing the researchers to demonstrate a cause-and-effect relationship as researchers manipulated the presence of testosterone to see its effect on aggressive behaviour.

An explanation of why testosterone and aggression are linked is the challenge hypothesis. This proposes that testosterone levels only rise above the base level in response to social challenges, such as threats to reproductive success. However, Mazur (1985) criticizes this explanation, claiming that individuals only act aggressively when their intention is to inflict injury; when their aim is to achieve status, they tend to act to assert dominance, which can be expressed in many different ways, of which aggression is only one. There is also a gender bias in research on testosterone and aggression, as research typically tends to concentrate only on the role of testosterone in males. However, Archer et al. (2005) found that the association between testosterone and aggression was even stronger for females. An additional problem for the role of testosterone in aggression is that research evidence is far from conclusive, with some studies showing no significant differences between violent and non-violent criminals (Bain et al. 1987), although another study found that the most violent criminals had higher testosterone levels than less violent criminals (Kreuz and Rose 1972). This suggests that among individuals who are already predisposed towards violence (e.g. because of genetics or social learning), testosterone may be an additional influence that makes aggressive behaviour more likely.

This is a mixture of AO1 and AO2, which is predominantly a discussion of the Kouri et al. study. This is accurate and detailed and the evaluative point appropriate and suitably elaborated.

This final paragraph begins with an explanation, which counts as AO1, but the rest of the paragraph is packed full of appropriate AO2 used in a highly effective manner and elaborated throughout. There is lots of intelligent comment that demonstrates a sound critical understanding of the area, including an intelligent IDA point made about gender bias.

**Strong answer: overall comment**

This is an excellent answer – well planned, well written, and offering a balanced discussion of both neural and hormonal mechanisms. This is a difficult topic, and the student has performed very well. This is a clear Grade A essay.

# Example Paper 2

## Question 1

### Part (a)

*Outline **one** social psychological theory of aggression.* [**5 marks** (2009 onwards)] [**4 marks** (2012 onwards)]

- Question 1 is in two parts. This part is entirely AO1. As you will see, the AO2 element is contained in part (b) below (along with some more AO1). You need to respond appropriately to the different requirements of the different parts.
- Part (a) requires you to outline just one social psychological theory of aggression. You would not get any credit for a second one.

- Sometimes questions include examples as part of the question (social learning theory, deindividuation, etc.), but that isn't the case here. You can choose whichever theory you like.
- There are only 5 marks available (4 marks 2012 onwards), so a short *descriptive* précis is required (about 100 to 120 words) and no evaluation.

#### Average answer

The social learning theory is explained by Bandura *et al.*, who carried out the famous Bobo doll study. In this study, children watched a film of an adult acting aggressively toward an inflatable doll. When the children were later allowed to play with the Bobo doll, they imitated the actions of the adult, using the same physical and verbal acts of aggression. In a variation of the study, the adult was either rewarded or punished by another adult for their aggression against the doll. Bandura found that when the adult was rewarded for their aggressive behaviour, the children imitated their behaviours, but not when they saw the child being punished for acting aggressively. Bandura used this study to develop his social learning theory.

This student has committed the classic error of describing a study when they should be describing a *theory*. This is a particular danger with social learning theory as many students can't get beyond describing the Bobo doll studies. To answer this question, the student should have used the insights from the study to develop an outline of the *theory*. For example, they might have stated that children observe the actions of aggressive models and are motivated to reproduce that behaviour because of vicarious reinforcement (i.e. seeing the model rewarded for their aggressive behaviour). As it is, this would only be worth about two or, at most, three of the five marks available.

#### Strong answer

The social learning theory of aggression stresses the importance of observational learning in the development of aggressive behaviour. Bandura *et al.*'s research showed we learn to be aggressive by observing the aggressive behaviour of those around us, particularly the behaviour of significant others. However, for the child to be motivated to reproduce this learned behaviour, it must be seen to be reinforcing for them. Bandura found that children are most likely to imitate aggressive behaviour if they see a significant other being rewarded for the same ☛

This is a much stronger answer. There is no mention of Bobo; instead, the student only draws implicitly on the underlying research. There are several concepts covered: observational learning, motivation, mental representation and expectation of reward. This answer is detailed and accurate, and is explicitly linked to aggressive behaviour throughout. It would be worth the full five marks.

behaviour (vicarious reinforcement). Children must also be able to form a mental representation of the aggressive behaviour, together with any associated rewards or punishments that are associated with it. It will then be reproduced, provided the expectation of reward is higher than the expectation of punishment.

## Part (b)

*Outline and evaluate the role of genetic factors in aggressive behaviour.* **[4 + 16 marks]**

Part (b) addresses a very different topic – genetic factors in aggressive behaviour. This also requires careful planning if you are not to slip up when answering it:

- Crucially, there are only 4 marks available for AO1, whereas there are 16 marks available for AO2. How do we know this? Whenever there is a split requirement (AO1 *and* AO2) in a parted question, the marks allocated to AO1 and AO2 are indicated *in that order*. Hence, 4 + 16 = 4 marks for AO1 and 16 for AO2. This means that you should plan your answer so that one-fifth of your content is AO1 description and four-fifths AO2 evaluation.
- Since part (b) requires an outline and evaluation of genetic factors in aggression, most of your content is likely to be based around research studies (e.g. twin studies). Simply describing a twin or adoption study would constitute AO1; to transform it into AO2, you would need to build in some form of commentary, e.g. 'The role of genetics in aggressive behaviour is supported by...'

### Average answer

Aggressive behaviour appears to run in families. For example, some studies have shown that violent criminals have violent fathers. Twin studies and adoption studies are the main way of researching the role of genetic factors in aggressive behaviour. A study by McGuffin and Gottesman found that the concordance rate for aggressive behaviour was over 80% for monozygotic twins (who share 100% of their genes) and just 70% for dizygotic twins (who share only 50% of their genes). A meta-analysis of 12 twin studies carried out by Mason and Frick concluded that about 50% of the individual differences in antisocial behaviour could be explained in terms of genetic factors. They also found that there was a larger genetic influence in violent antisocial behaviours than in nonviolent antisocial behaviours.

The second type of study is the adoption study. This involves studying individuals who have not been brought up by their biological parents. A study in Denmark by Hutchings and Mednick found a significant positive ☞

This is all accurate and detailed, but as yet, entirely descriptive. This is fine *provided* whatever follows is all AO2, as there are only 4 marks available for AO1 and 16 for AO2.

correlation between the number of convictions for violent behaviours between biological parents and their adopted sons. A meta-analysis of twin and adoption studies by Miles and Carey (1997) found that approximately 50% of the variance in aggression could be accounted for in terms of genetics. They also found that the importance of genetics in aggressive behaviour increased with age and the importance of environmental factors decreased.

There has also been research into the role that particular genes might play in the development of aggression. One of the genes thought to influence aggression is MAOA, which stands for monoamine oxidase A. MAOA breaks down neurotransmitters such as dopamine, which are associated with aggressive behaviour. A study in the Netherlands found that a family where there were many violent individuals all had a defective gene for MAOA, and as a result had low levels of MAOA. The researchers concluded that because there were low levels of MAOA in these individuals, this means that they had high levels of the neurotransmitters that lead to aggressive behaviour.

There are problems with a lot of these studies. For example, in twin studies, there is no way of knowing how much of the similarity between twins is due to genetic similarity or environmental factors. Some critics believe that MZ twins share a more similar environment anyway, because they tend to be treated as 'the twins' rather than separate individuals. There is also the problem that if aggressive behaviour was entirely due to genetic factors, then there would be a concordance rate of 100% for MZ twins. However, it is only 50%, so this means that environmental factors are as important as genetic factors. An alternative explanation is the social learning theory, which explains aggression in terms of the individual imitating the behaviour of violent role models and then being motivated to reproduce that behaviour if they associate it with reinforcement.

As feared, the student has continued to describe studies of the relationship between genes and aggression rather than using these studies to construct a critical evaluation of the genetic perspective. There is a fine line between merely describing a study and using it critically. For example, the student might have continued the sentence about Hutchings and Mednick's study by adding: '… *thus supporting the influence of genetic factors in violent behaviour as this correlation cannot be attributed to environmental factors because these individuals do not experience shared environments.*' The addition of the italicized material turns the whole study into an effective AO2 point.

We finally have some explicitly evaluative material, but there is far too little of it, given the number of marks available for AO2. A couple of decent critical points are made, although the 'alternative explanation' given at the end is not used in an evaluative way, being nothing more than extra (and largely irrelevant) description. It could have been made relevant by showing that it offers something that genetic explanations cannot. A serious problem for this answer is the total absence of IDA material, which will depress the marks even more.

**Average answer: overall comment**

There is *far* too much AO1 material in this second part of the answer and *far* too little AO2. The student may have left the exam hall feeling that they have done a good job, but this answer would earn low marks because of the relative absence of AO2 and IDA material. It would struggle to reach a pass standard. There is a very important lesson to learn in this answer: always plan your answers so that they reflect the division of AO1 and AO2 stated in the question.

**Strong answer**

The role of genetics in aggressive behaviour has been studied by comparing MZ with DZ twins – any greater similarity (measured by the concordance rate) in terms of aggressive behaviour between MZ twins can be assumed to be a result of their greater genetic similarity. For example, a study by McGuffin and Gottesman (1985) found a concordance rate for aggressive behaviour of 87% for MZ twins and 72% for DZ twins. This finding is supported by a meta-analysis of 12 twin studies (Mason and Frick 1994), who concluded that approximately half of the influence on aggressive behaviour appeared to be due to genetic factors, and that there was a greater genetic influence in more violent behaviours. Studies such as this do support the genetic claim, but because DZ twins (who share only 50% of their genes) have such a high degree of similarity, this suggests that a shared environment also exerts a powerful influence. This is highlighted by the fact that MZ twins tend to share a more 'similar' environment than do DZ twins, as they tend to be treated in more similar ways than are DZ twins, and this could account for their higher concordance rate for aggressive behaviour. A further meta-analysis of twin studies (Miles and Carey 1997) also supported the role of genetic factors in aggression, but challenged the view that environmental factors have the same influence across the lifespan. They concluded that as people reach adulthood, the influence of the rearing environment decreases and the influences of genes increases.

Adoption studies have the advantage of removing the influence of a shared environment and offering the opportunity to study the influence of shared genetics when reared apart. For example, Hutchings and Mednick (1973) reviewed over 14 000 adoptions in Denmark. They found a significant positive correlation between the number of convictions for criminal violence among adopted sons and their biological fathers. There is, however, a problem with interpreting findings such as this. For example, in some countries, children who are given up for adoption display a higher rate of antisocial behaviour at the time of their adoption. Tremblay (2003) claims that parents who give up their children for adoption also display higher rates of antisocial behaviour than is the case with adoptive parents. This makes it difficult to disentangle the effects of nature and nurture when interpreting the results of adoption studies. ☞

This is a very effective and carefully executed paragraph. It is restricted to twin studies, but also limits the descriptive content to almost exactly one quarter of the paragraph (exactly as it should be). Everything else after the sentence ending '…72 per cent for DZ twins' is AO2, and the student is careful to use phrases such as 'This finding is supported by…', '…also supported by' and '…but challenged the view that', to ensure that this material receives AO2 rather than AO1 credit. Drawing conclusions and interpreting studies would also count as AO2, but making this explicit makes sure that the material is credited in this way. In questions such as this, where there is such a big difference in the number of AO1 and AO2 marks available, examiners will be sympathetic, but you can help them to help you by 'flagging' your AO2 in this way (i.e. using AO2 terms).

As with the previous paragraph, there is an obvious division into AO1 and AO2, with the first three sentences again being the AO1 content and the remainder the AO2. This time the student has looked at the methodological problems associated with twin and adoption studies, and has carefully used the terms 'nature' and 'nurture' as they highlight the possibility of gene–environment interactions. In this way, they are satisfying the IDA requirement of the question.

There is also the problem of gene–environment interaction. It is possible that individuals with a genetic propensity for aggressive behaviour seek out aggressive experiences, and that any resulting aggressive behaviour is a product of both these influences. Interactions between genes and environment may influence aggressive behaviour in other ways as well.

There are some positive applications of genetic research on aggression. For example, Morley and Hall (2003) suggest that information obtained from genetic screenings may be used to identify individuals who are likely to commit violent crimes, and appropriate treatments developed to help these individuals. However, this raises the problem of whether a genetic predisposition for violent behaviour might be used to reduce a person's criminal responsibility for their behaviour, because, according to this determinist view of aggressive behaviour, a violent offender cannot be assumed to possess free will, and therefore cannot be held morally responsible for their behaviour.

This final paragraph is entirely AO2 (real-life application *and* a discussion of the free will versus determinism debate) and would also count as IDA. This rounds the essay off nicely and is a clear indication of someone who has thought carefully about the structure of their essay rather than simply throwing everything at the page and hoping some of it is relevant.

### Strong answer: overall comment

With a careful balance of AO1 and AO2 material, a well-structured argument that includes relevant research, and good IDA material embedded into the flow of the text, this is a very competent answer and a clear Grade A.

## Question 2

*Discuss explanations of institutional aggression.* [**25 marks** (2009 onwards)] [**24 marks** (2012 onwards)]

- This *should* be a pretty straightforward question to answer. There is a requirement for both AO1 and AO2 (as there is in all questions) and the split is 9/16 (8/16 from 2012 onwards).
- The question asks for 'explanations' in the plural, so at least two explanations need to be covered. If you only discuss one, you will limit the number of marks you can score.
- Remember that you are trying to *explain* institutional aggression, not just describe it. Research can be used to elaborate explanations or to provide evidence that supports (or challenges) these explanations.

- AQA don't specify exactly what constitutes 'institutional aggression', but in this book we have defined it as aggression between individuals *within* institutions (such as prisons or similar institutions) and aggression between members of *different* institutions (e.g. racial or political groups). If you decide to write about the latter type in an exam, it would be prudent to justify why it constitutes *institutional* aggression.
- If you try to cover too many explanations in your answer, there is the danger that your answer will lack detail and elaboration (AO2); two or three is usually a good number, allowing you to address the requirements of the question while maintaining a sufficient level of depth in your answer.

### Average answer

The three main explanations of institutional aggression are the importation model which claims that aggression in places like prisons is due to the fact that there are lots of violent individuals there; the deprivation model, which claims that institutions make people violent because they deprive them of privacy and other needs; and the deindividuation model, which claims that people lose their sense of individual responsibility in institutions and this makes them more likely to behave in an antisocial manner.

A good opening paragraph, concise and clear and piling up the AO1 marks already. However, there is a danger that, by describing these models in such a concise way early on, any subsequent description will be repetitive and will not earn any more marks. However, a good start.

The importation model claims that many of the people who end up in prison come from violent or poor backgrounds where violence is more acceptable, and so they bring these characteristics with them into prison. Violence is then seen as an appropriate way to resolve conflicts while in prison. This is supported by a study by Adams (1981), who found that Black inmates in US prisons display more violent behaviour toward other prisoners, and this is thought to reflect the cultural norms of the poor communities that many Black prisoners come from. However, a study by DeLisi *et al.* (2004) found no evidence that being a member of a violent gang prior to prison had any influence on violent behaviour among those individuals when they went to prison. The deprivation model argues that the experience of prison (e.g. overcrowding, noise and a lack of any meaningful activity) means that inmates ☞

This is again concise, but has a good mix of AO1 and AO2 material, with studies used sensibly to form a critical commentary on both importation and deprivation models. It does need fleshing out, though. The student should have anticipated a question such as this and had more to write about both models. For example, they may have described the particular types of traits that might be imported and looked a little deeper at the nature of the deprivation that occurs in institutions such as prisons. Similarly, the evaluation might have been elaborated a little more. We are told, for example, that the McCorkle *et al.* study fails to support the main claims of the model, but no other information about this is given.

are more likely to respond with violence toward other inmates. In UK prisons, for example, overcrowding has meant that many prisoners are forced to share cells, which reduces their personal space and makes violent behaviour more likely. However, although some studies have supported the deprivation model, many others have not. For example, one of the largest studies in this area (McCorkle *et al.* 1995) failed to support the main claims of the model. McCorkle also points out that the deprivation associated with imprisonment is constant, yet outbreaks of violent behaviour are sporadic.

Zimbardo claims that when people are in institutions such as prison or the military, there is a greater chance of them becoming deindividuated. This is increased when uniforms are worn (by the guards) and prisoners lose their sense of personal identity and become numbers. Zimbardo's Stanford Prison Experiment demonstrated that, when there is a lack of supervision and no clear guidelines for behaviour, this deindividuation process becomes even more likely. He found that his 'guards' were more likely to behave aggressively toward the prisoners in such situations. There is a real-life application of this idea, in an understanding of the prisoner abuses at Abu Ghraib prison in Iraq. There were many similarities with the Stanford Prison Experiment, and deindividuation and lack of supervision was clearly evident.

> The concise theme continues in this final paragraph. The student might have indicated in more detail the relationship between deindividuation and institutional aggression, and could have made more explicit comparisons with the Abu Ghraib prisoner abuses. However, this does serve as IDA material, so, although there isn't much of it, that requirement is covered.

### Average answer: overall comment

This is a fairly typical response to a question where a student feels they do not know that much. However, this topic is clearly marked on the specification, and, as about 600 words are expected for a good, detailed response, the student should have thought of ways to add detail and elaboration. However, the answer is accurate and appropriate, and even though only around 450 words, it would still be worth a Grade C.

**Strong answer**

Institutional aggression is commonplace in prisons. Research by the Howard League for Penal Reform (2009) has shown that the incident of violent acts has risen by a third in the last five years. The importation model (Irwin and Cressey 1962) argues that prisoners bring their own social histories and characteristics into prison, and so are already violent when they enter prison. Younger inmates are thought to have more difficulties adjusting to the transition into prison and are therefore more prone to interpersonal violence. Clear *et al.* (2009) explain this as partly because young males have greater physical strength than older inmates, but also because many young males have problems defining their position in society and are therefore likely to see many interactions as challenges to their status. The importation model is supported by research by Harer and Steffensmeier (2006), who studied incident statistics in 58 US prisons. They found that Black inmates had significantly higher rates of violent behaviour but lower alcohol and drug-related misconduct compared to White inmates. These statistics reflected social trends outside prison, thus supporting the claim that social and culturally determined characteristics are imported into the prison environment. The model is also supported by research by Keller and Wang (2005), who found that prison violence is more likely to occur in prisons that hold maximum-security inmates, with assaults on staff and other inmates more common than in prisons with lower-security inmates. The deprivation model argues that institutional aggression in prisons or other institutions such as mental hospitals is a product of the stressful and oppressive conditions in those institutions (e.g. isolation from friends and family, boredom and overcrowding). Overcrowding has been shown to increase aggressive behaviour because it cuts down psychological space and privacy. The overcrowding crisis in UK prisons has led to an increase in interpersonal violence and even suicides. Lack of staff experience is also linked to increased interpersonal aggression. For example, Davies and Burgess found that less-experienced prison officers were more likely to be the victim of assaults. There is research evidence to support the claims that deprivation in institutions leads to aggressive behaviour. McCorkle *et al.* (1995) found that overcrowding, lack of privacy and lack of meaningful activity all contributed to violence in a prison setting. However, this is not true across all institutions, with research by ☞

A very effective paragraph that is one-third description and two-thirds evaluation. There is a clear and accurate description of the importation model with appropriate elaboration of its central claims. The AO1 material is plentiful and well developed. For example, we have an explanation as to why younger inmates are more likely to be involved in interpersonal violence. The rest of the AO2 material is supporting research evidence that is perfectly appropriate and shows a good critical understanding of the area.

The paragraph on the deprivation model also shows a detailed description of the main characteristics of institutional deprivation and explains why these would be likely to lead to increased interpersonal aggression. There is excellent critical commentary on the model, with good use of research evidence and argument to support the claims being made. Wilson's use of these insights in a real-world setting (HMP Woodhill) counts as part of the IDA response (although this is credited as AO2).

Nijman *et al.* finding that increasing personal space made no difference to interpersonal violence in a psychiatric setting. Research in this area has been applied in a real-world attempt to change levels of aggressive behaviour in prisons. Most violence occurs in environments that are hot, noise polluted (e.g. shouting, banging cell doors) and overcrowded (prison population increasing year on year). Wilson (2005) reduced levels of crowding, heat and noise at HMP Woodhill, which in turn led to a dramatic decrease in violent behaviour among inmates.

Institutional aggression is also evident in other settings such as the army or in universities, where initiation rituals (or 'hazing') occur, whereby group members within an institution cause another group member to suffer rituals that are abusive, humiliating or harmful. It is sometimes difficult to define when such behaviours become 'aggressive' rather than harmless fun. Many of the victims of such rituals do not report it because they do not recognise it as abusive or aggressive behaviour. This type of institutional aggression has been found in the military (Winslow 2004) and in prisons (McCorkle 1992). McCorkle found that in prisons, domination of the weak was seen as essential to maintaining status among inmates, with passive behaviour seen as weakness and likely to invite exploitation. Research has appeared to suggest that hazing is initiated mainly by males and that males tend to be the victims. However, this demonstrates a gender bias in the interpretation of hazing. Men appear both to use and be the victims of physical hazing acts, whereas women often show a preference for more psychological and emotional hazing acts (Nuwer 1999). However, acts of psychological hazing may be more difficult to recognize because they do not leave observable effects in the way that acts of physical hazing usually do.

This final explanation of institutional aggression (centred around initiation rituals) is described appropriately without the unnecessary detailing of the different types of initial rituals that have characterized this type of aggression. The use of research evidence is appropriately evaluative, and there is an excellent IDA point about the gender bias associated with research in this area, which also explains *why* hazing tends to be associated with males rather than females.

**Strong answer: overall comment**

An excellent answer, lots of good material and an entirely appropriate balance between AO1 and AO2 material. This is a clear Grade A standard answer.

## Question 3

*Discuss **two or more** evolutionary explanations of group display in humans.*
[**25 marks** (2009 onwards)] [**24 marks** (2012 onwards)]

- As with the previous question, this question requires a minimum of two explanations of a psychological phenomenon – in this case, 'group display'. As this topic is in a section of the specification on aggression as an 'adaptive response', the approach we have taken in this book is to look at how group behaviours have evolved because they serve an adaptive purpose. This gives you the opportunity to provide *explanations* for group display, rather than just describing the different ways that groups behave. This is important, because there is a clear temptation to spend too long detailing the violent behaviour of football crowds or the 'strange' behaviours of religious fundamentalists, without ever actually explaining them.

- The question invites you to write about 'two or more' explanations; it is for you to decide how many explanations to write about. Some students can fill their answer with appropriate material from just two, while others need more than two to get up to about 600 words or so. The choice is yours, but more explanations does not necessarily mean more marks. In fact, more explanations can mean *fewer* marks if your treatment of each becomes superficial.

- Finally, a cautionary note about one word that may well be missed, i.e. 'humans'. Sometimes, teachers like to illustrate evolutionary principles (e.g. natural and sexual selection) by referring to non-human animals. This is a perfectly appropriate way of explaining a principle or theory, but if the exam question asks you to explain group display in *humans*, then you must restrict your answer to that – material on non-humans will not gain marks.

### Average answer

The first type of group display is the behaviour of sports crowd. Football crowds in particular have become more and more violent over the last fifty years or so, and are also associated with their racist and xenophobic chants. In one famous incident in 2006, Samuel Eto'o, while he was playing for Barcelona, threatened to leave the pitch because he was being subjected to racist chants by the Real Zaragoza supporters. Play had to be stopped and an announcement was made to the crowd asking for the abuse to stop. There are many reasons why sports crowds act in this way toward outsiders. It is believed, for example, that xenophobic chants hark back to our ancestors' mistrust of outsiders, and so this form of group display is a way of forging solidarity with other group members by showing hostility toward outsiders. It is better to be suspicious of outsiders because that way, humans are prepared for any attack. There is evidence to support this. In one study the researchers looked at football matches involving the England team in Europe and matches involving club teams. They found that there was a lot more evidence of xenophobic displays from foreign supporters toward the national side than toward club sides. The evolutionary ☞

This is an interesting but not particularly effective paragraph for several reasons. There is too much descriptive detail about the Samuel Eto'o example, and the description of the adaptive nature of football crowd behaviours and displays is a bit woolly. The AO2 material is relevant, although a little too restricted. It is not used particularly effectively either – for example, the student describes a supporting study (Marsh), but doesn't tell us how or why this supports an evolutionary explanation of these displays.

explanation is criticized by Marsh, who studied group displays of violence among football supporters. He claims that football hooligans use football violence and racist chants as a sort of career, rising from 'foot soldiers' to 'lieutenants'. He claims there is no evolutionary significance to these displays other than as a way of achieving status within their group.

The second type of group display is religious displays. Sosis explains that religious groups can perform very costly ritualistic displays, like flagellation and fasting, because by whole groups engaging in costly rituals, it makes it less likely that other people will try to take the benefits offered by that group without committing to its ideals. Sosis uses the example of ultra orthodox Jewish males who wear long beards and heavy coats in the middle of an Israeli summer, which must be very uncomfortable for them, but acts as a way of signalling their level of commitment to their faith and at the same time deterring others who may try to take the benefits of group membership. They would be deterred because commitment would be seen as too costly. Displays are therefore seen as a way of increasing cooperation within a group and decreasing invasion from outsiders. Sosis found evidence to support this with an analysis of synagogue attendance. He found a positive correlation between synagogue attendance and the level of cooperative behaviour in males. One of the problems with an evolutionary explanation is that increases in intergroup solidarity using religious displays are often accompanied by increased intergroup hostility. There is evidence to suggest that societies that have the strictest religious displays also experience the highest levels of intergroup conflict (Sosis *et al.*). They also found that these societies often insisted on very painful ritual scars for males to deter these males from leaving that society and going to another one.

This is a much more effective paragraph. There is a clear and informative description of *why* religious groups engage in costly displays, although the explanation is repeated (in slightly different words) several times. Sosis' research is used to good effect both to detail the descriptive content (e.g. the example of orthodox Jewish males wearing heavy coats in summer) and to build a critical evaluation of the content. There is a discussion of the problems with an evolutionary perspective of intragroup cooperation, which just about satisfies the need to have some IDA content.

## Average answer: overall comment

This is a difficult area, and the student has made a decent attempt to cover two separate explanations in order to satisfy the requirements of the question. However, the evaluation would need to be better developed, given that double the marks are available for AO2 compared to AO1. The essay is around Grade C/D standard.

**Strong answer**

Some group-based behavioural displays may confer an adaptive advantage for the individuals within those groups and may, therefore, arise in particular social situations. The behaviour of sports crowds is one such example. Natural selection favours the evolution of characteristics that cause individuals to behave cooperatively toward other group members but view outsiders suspiciously (xenophobia). Van Vught *et al.* (2007) also propose that among human beings, a 'tribal psychology' has evolved, which increases their propensity for outgroup disparagement and hostility and the dehumanization of non-group members. These behaviours can be seen in the hostile and dehumanizing chants and banners of football supporters.

There is research support for the claim that xenophobic group displays are common among football crowds. Foldesi (1996) studied football crowds in Hungary and found evidence of many racist and xenophobic displays, in the form of chants and banners. These displays were aimed at groups considered to be 'outsiders', such as Blacks, Jews, Gypsies and Russians. Evans and Rowe (2002) also found evidence of xenophobic displays in a study of football crowds in continental Europe that involved either the English national team or English club sides. They found that xenophobic chants and banners directed towards the English teams were more common when it was the England team than club sides. They concluded that club sides, because they are more ethnically and culturally diverse than the national team, were less likely to provoke xenophobic outbursts in opposition supporters. The tendency of sports crowds toward xenophobic displays has prompted some football clubs to take active steps to prevent it. For example, relations between Glasgow Celtic (Catholic) and Glasgow Rangers (Protestant) have long been blighted by sectarian displays of bigotry and xenophobia. Celtic have initiated the 'Bhoys against Bigotry' campaign, where sectarian chants and banners are forbidden, e.g. by banning the singing of provocative IRA songs on the terraces. In England, many clubs have started football clinics for minorities and have taken initiatives to stamp out racism on the terraces.

Painful and costly ritual religious displays appear to contradict the rules of natural selection, i.e. that behaviours would only evolve if they confer an ☞

Description of the adaptive nature of group displays among sports crowds is concise but accurate, and avoids the trap of including too much 'contextual' detail. The emphasis is on *explaining* the behaviour of sports crowds rather than simply chronicling it. Compare this with the opening paragraph of the 'Average answer' on p. 64 – this is much more effective.

This is a difficult area to be truly evaluative, but this student has managed it – and managed it well. Evidence is used sensibly to show where studies (e.g. Foldesi) support the claim that many of the group displays found among sports crowds are xenophobic. The Evans and Rowe study is used as evaluation, but, unlike the 'Average answer', its relevance as evaluation is made clear. Antisectarian and antiracist initiatives are introduced as real-world application, and this counts as IDA material, which again is used effectively.

adaptive advantage on the individual. Therefore, costly group displays must be advantageous in some way, possibly because they encourage cooperation among members of the group. By engaging in costly displays, such as ritual self-flagellation, the individual signals their commitment to the group, but also signals that they are likely to cooperate with other groups members for the benefit of the whole group. The use of costly ritualistic displays has an additional value, as it deters outsiders from taking the benefits offered by group membership without committing to the group and working toward group goals.

Evidence to support the 'costly signalling theory' comes from Ruffle and Sosis (2005) in a study of Israeli communes. They found that more religious males were also more cooperative towards other members of the commune. This was not the case with females. They claim that this is because males must engage in more costly and more highly visible ritual requirements, including frequent episodes of public prayer. These results are consistent with the prediction that more conspicuous displays are related to higher levels of cooperation within the group. Sosis et al. (2005) tested the prediction that costly male ritualistic displays evolved to signal group commitment among males who must cooperate in warfare. They carried out an analysis of 60 societies to determine whether the frequency of warfare was in some way linked to the costs of group rituals. They found that the nature of warfare in those societies determined the type of ritualistic display. In societies where the main threat was external, group members performed more permanent displays of commitment (e.g. scars and incisions) to signal their commitment to that group. In societies where the threat was more internal (i.e. groups form and break up frequently within that society), group displays of commitment tend to be less permanent (e.g. body painting or adornments) as individuals may be less willing to commit to one group permanently. These explanations, however, apply almost entirely to males and therefore tell us very little about the reasons why females may engage in group displays. As such, they offer a gender-biased analysis of this behaviour.

This is a detailed and accurate explanation of what Zahavi refers to as 'costly signalling theory'. The two main claims of this theory – that it fosters cooperation and deters free-riders – are explained clearly and concisely.

Here, evaluative material is clearly related to the theory described in the previous paragraph. With weaker answers, examiners often struggle to understand why a particular point constitutes critical commentary of the AO1 material, but this student has chosen material carefully and makes its links with the AO1 descriptive material explicit. For example, when introducing the Sosis et al. study, this student states that 'Sosis et al. (2005) tested the prediction that…'. There is plenty of elaboration and a good spread of points made. The answer ends with a discussion of possible gender bias in this explanation, fulfilling the IDA requirement of the question in a detailed and effective manner.

## Strong answer: overall comment

An excellent answer, with lots of good material and an entirely appropriate balance between AO1 and AO2 material. This is a very good response to a difficult subject area and is a clear Grade A standard answer.

# Glossary

**Adaptive response**   An evolved behaviour (or trait) that increases the likelihood of the individual's survival and successful reproduction

**ADHD (attention deficit hyperactivity disorder)**   A common childhood disorder that can continue through adolescence and adulthood; symptoms include difficulty staying focused and paying attention, difficulty controlling behaviour and hyperactivity (overactivity)

**Altruism**   Helping another person with no personal gain and some cost to the person doing the helping

**Amphetamines**   A group of drugs that stimulate the central nervous system; used legally in the treatment of various disorders, including depression, but also abused illegally as a stimulant

**Amygdala**   The part of the brain that controls fear, anger and other emotional responses

**Androgen hormones**   Hormones, such as testosterone, that produce male characteristics

**Anthropological**   Relating to anthropology, the study of people and their cultures

**Bobo doll**   A large inflatable plastic doll used by Bandura and colleagues in their research on aggression

**Candidate gene**   A gene suspected of being involved in the expression of a trait, such as a disease

**Concordance rate**   In a sample of twin pairs, the concordance rate refers to the number of times one twin shows, for instance, the same particular disorder as the other twin. In a sample of 200 pairs of twins, if 90 have the disorder, then the concordance rate is 45 per cent

**Correlational data**   Data that show an association between two variables (but not a cause-and-effect relationship)

**Cortisol**   A hormone released in response to stress

**Credibility enhancing displays (CREDs)**   Observable behaviours (displays) that provide other group members with a reliable indication of the model's actual degree of commitment to the beliefs that they have expressed verbally

**Cuckoldry**   When a woman deceives her partner into investing in (e.g. providing for, protecting) offspring conceived with another man

**Dehumanization**   Stripping a person or group of their individuality or identity, and thereby viewing them as less than human

**Deindividuation**   Process that occurs when one loses one's sense of individual identity so that social, moral and societal constraints on behaviour are loosened

**Demand characteristics**   Features of a research situation that participants perceive they must respond to, sometimes leading to changes in behaviour that become a source of extraneous variation in the study

**Dependent variable**   In an experiment, the variable that is assumed to be directly affected by changes in the independent variable. In a well-designed experiment, any changes in the dependent variable are presumed to have been caused by the independent variable

**Determinism**   The philosophical doctrine that an individual's behaviour is shaped or controlled by internal or external forces rather than an individual's own free will

**Dominance**   Having status over or controlling other individuals

**Dopamine**   A neurotransmitter (a chemical messenger used to transmit impulses from one nerve cell to another). The overactivity of dopamine has been linked to schizophrenia

**Ethical issues**   Issues that arise in research where there is a conflict between the rights and dignity of participants and the goals and outcomes of research (e.g. in Zimbardo's Stanford Prison Experiment, the issue of whether participants should have been protected from harm)

**Free will**   The philosophical doctrine that individuals are capable of making their own choices, i.e. that they are self-determining and free from coercion

**Impulsivity**   A personality trait characterized by the tendency to initiate behaviour without thinking about the consequences of any actions, acting on the spur of the moment; impulsivity has been shown to be a major component of various neuropsychiatric disorders such as ADHD

**Independent variable**   In an experiment, the variable manipulated by the experimenter that is presumed to have a direct effect on the dependent variable

**Infidelity**   Unfaithfulness, e.g. sexual infidelity – when a man or a woman has sexual relations with someone other than their partner

**Institutional aggression**   Violent behaviour that exists within, and may be a defining feature of, certain institutions and groups. It can also refer to other forms of collective violence *between* social groups (such as the violent behaviour observed in riots and intergroup conflict)

**Intergroup**   Between groups, e.g. intergroup aggression is aggression that takes place between different groups

**Intragroup**   Within a group, e.g. intragroup solidarity is solidarity between members of a group

**Inverse correlation**   An association between two variables, whereby scores on one variable increase as scores on the other decrease

**Jealousy**   A state of fear or suspicion caused by a real or imagined threat to one's current status, e.g. in males, their status as an exclusive sexual partner, leading to sexual jealousy

**Laboratory experiment**   An experiment carried out in a laboratory, allowing the researcher to exert a high level of control over the independent variable, and to eliminate or control for confounding variables

**Longitudinal study**   The study of an individual or group of individuals at regular intervals over a relatively long period of time

**Meta-analysis**   A method of combining a number of studies on the same theme in order to detect trends in the behaviour being studied; this technique is often used in systematic reviews

**Monogamous**   Being married to only one partner at a time

**Natural selection**   The part of Darwin's theory that states that animals that are well adapted to their environment will leave behind more offspring than animals that are less well adapted

**Neurotransmitters**   The chemicals which allow the transmission of signals from one neuron to the next across synapses

**Normative cues**   Aspects of a social situation that give cues – whether subtle or overt – as to what is 'normal' or expected in terms of behaviour

**Operant conditioning**   An explanation of learning that sees the consequences of behaviour as of vital importance to the future appearance of that behaviour. If a behaviour is followed by a desirable consequence, it becomes more frequent; if it is followed by an undesirable consequence, it becomes less frequent

**PET (positron emission tomography) scans**
A non-invasive technique for visualizing (imaging) the activity in the brain by measuring the accumulation of a radioactive substance in various regions of the brain. A battery of detectors scans the brain after the radioactive substance has been injected into the bloodstream

**Prefrontal cortex**    Area at the front of the brain responsible for the executive functions, such as mediating conflicting thoughts, making choices between right and wrong, and governing social control (e.g. suppressing emotional or sexual urges)

**Presynaptic neurons**    Neurons situated in front of the synapse

**Postsynaptic receptors**    Cells on the surface of neurons situated after a synapse, which receive serotonin and are stimulated by it

**Prosocial**    Describing behaviour that benefits others but which may appear to have no direct benefit for the person displaying it

**Reproductive fitness**    A measure of the success of an individual in passing on their genes to the next generation and beyond

**Schizophrenia**    A serious mental disorder that is characterized by severe disruptions in psychological functioning and a loss of contact with reality

**Scripts**    A sequence of expected behaviours for a given situation, learned by observation of others, habit, practice and routine. For example, when an individual enters a restaurant they choose a table, order, wait, eat, pay the bill, and leave

**Self-efficacy**    An individual's expectation of reward and confidence in their ability to use a particular behaviour effectively (e.g. aggression)

**Serotonin**    A neurotransmitter (a chemical messenger used to transmit impulses from one nerve cell to another). Abnormal activity of serotonin has been linked to depression and OCD

**Serotonin metabolism**    Chemical reactions at the synapse involving serotonin

**Sexual coercion**    Using physical force (e.g. rape) and/or psychological pressure (e.g. threats of violence or promise of favours) to compel someone to engage in sexual activity

**Sexual selection**    The observation that individuals possess features that make them attractive to members of the opposite sex (intersexual selection), or help them to compete with members of the same sex for access to mates (intrasexual selection)

**Social desirability bias**    In research studies, a tendency for participants to respond in a way that will be viewed favourably by others

**Social learning theory**    An explanation of the way in which people learn by observing and imitating the behaviour of others, mentally rehearsing the behaviours and then later imitating them in similar situations

**SSRI (Selective Serotonin Reuptake Inhibitors)**
Drugs that focus purely on serotonin, blocking the reuptake of serotonin from the synaptic cleft (the best known of these drugs is probably Prozac). SSRIs seem to enhance energy and are used to treat depression

**Stanford Prison Experiment**    A classic experiment carried out by Zimbardo *et al.* (1973), designed to study the psychological effects of becoming a prisoner or prison guard. Participants were assigned the roles of either prisoner and guard in a realistic prison setting, with the 'guards' exhibiting brutal behaviour and the 'prisoners' becoming passive and subservient

**Synapse**    In the nervous system, a junction that permits a neuron to transmit signals to another cell

**Vicarious reinforcement**    Learning how to behave by seeing other people being rewarded or punished for a particular (e.g. aggressive) behaviour

**Xenophobia**    Suspicion or fear of strangers

# Index